I, CLODHOPPER!

an agricultural getaway

ISBN
978-1-6866059-5-6
LLCN: XTK

I, CLODHOPPER!

an agricultural getaway

STEPHEN M. ARCHER

2019

The author at an early age considering his future. Note the steely gaze and the air of suspicion, left fist at the ready. Nice hair, though. From the author's collection.

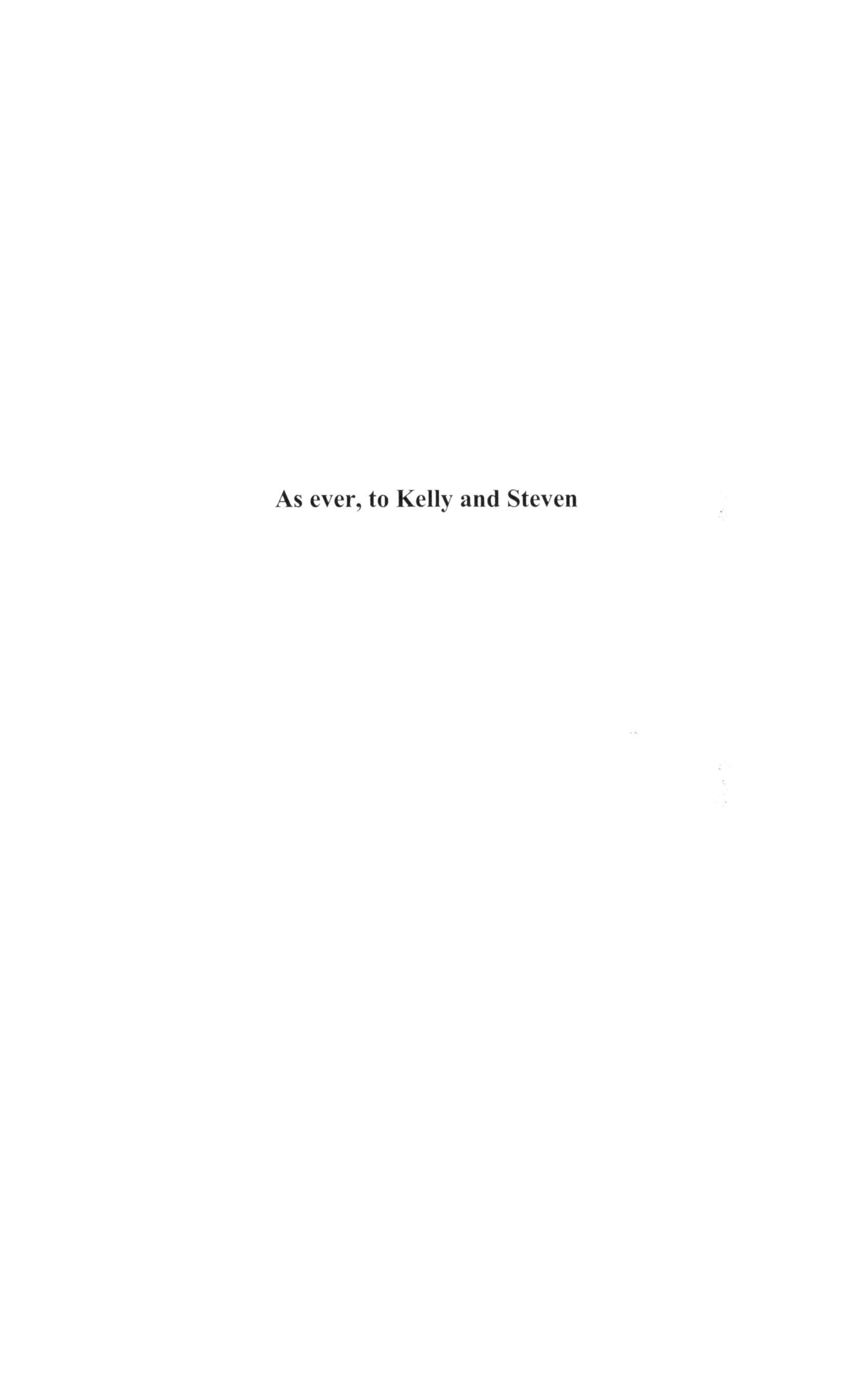

As ever, to Kelly and Steven

“Try as we might, we write what we write.”

–bg Thurston

CONTENTS

CHAPTER ONE

ENTER, STAGE RIGHT, UNARMED, OR, EXISTENCE PRECEDES ESSENSE

I was born and raised on a family farm in the middle of this country, but I'll be a suck-egg mule if I take the blame for that. I mean, like, it wasn't my fault.

After The Parents checked my plumbing, dried me off, and swaddled me into rigidity they lugged me off to an eighty-acre rented farm, where I grew to whelpdom. And it took me about twenty-five years to get off that farm.

When I became self-propelled and began to investigate my surroundings, I discovered not much of it interested me. I soon came not so much to dislike that farm as to seek other venues.

So I started pretty early imagining other ways to live. And in due time I found some. Not, however, before I passed through The Twelve Stages of Asininity. I did hard time as:

1. A student. Ranging from sluggish to marginal.
2. A Coca-Cola bottler. Two weeks @ 40¢ an hour.
3. A gravedigger. Picks and shovels. 108°. Sweaty.
4. A pool hustler. A very short career.

5. An actor. Had to quit, bad for my health.
6. A bootlegger. An even shorter career than #4.
7. Maintenance of a city baseball park. Not bad.
8. A truck rental agency. A dick for a boss.
9. A filling station attendant. A pervert in charge.
10. A janitor. In a high school, no less.
11. A sound technician. Great fun.
12. A maker of crayons for little kiddies. 27 months.

This list hints at how much I wanted to leave that farm. Kids notoriously crave to leave home; they seek to enter the adult world and have more fun. That creaky cliché contains a nugget of truth, at least in the United States, a nation mostly descended from fiddle-footed emigrants.

That truism further suggests almost everyone yearns to go somewhere else, over the hill to the next horizon. They might find that horizon on the moon, or in Prague, or in some library stacks, or in Oblong, Illinois, depending on how their crumbling cookie crumbled. We may like to think of ourselves as in charge of things, but as the Stoics say, first we have to determine what we can do something about and second what we cannot. I think they got that right. A friend of mine once told me that all human endeavor falls in one of two categories: his problems, and everybody else's problems. He was edging up on How Things Are, I think. Epictetus (ca. AD 50—135), a Greek-speaking Stoic philosopher, nailed it when he said in his *Discourses:*

> *The chief task in life is simply this: to identify and separate matters so that I can say clearly to myself which are externals not under my control, and which have to do with the choices I actually control. Where then do I look for good and evil?*

Not to uncontrollable externals, but within myself to the choices that are my own. . . .
Discourses, 2.5.4-5

And lest we forget, Epictetus had the good fortune to enjoy Marcus Aurelius for a student. You'll meet him later, but forget about that movie, *The Gladiator.*

Act One, Scene One

So begins this remembrance of times passed. I made my first entrance and found myself in an agricultural circumstance, blinking like an actor suddenly finding himself in a spotlight. Since for some misguided years I considered myself an actor, that metaphor may serve now.

The great Russian theatre director Konstantin Stanislavski (1863-1938) proposed that actors should know their situation before attempting to enact it: the time, the specific place, from whence the character comes, their intentions, etc. Many actors still follow his advice; some do not.

ASIDE: Stanislavski became widely known among undergraduates in and around St. Louis as "Stan the Man." It figures.

I'm including these ASIDES in lieu of footnotes, which make readers crazy. Actors sometimes address the audience directly from the stage; they call doing that an "aside." You don't have to read mine, but I hope you do.

Stanislavski called his concept "The Given Circumstances." Mediocre actors don't bother with this homework; it seems too much trouble, like grammar for a would-be writer or scales for a beginning musician. And even though actors may do detailed analyses of their scenes they may still stink out loud in performance. But it gives them a place to start, and some of the better performers use it.

I submit The Given Circumstances for my first entrance:

TIME: Mid-May, 1934, about daybreak, during the Great Depression. The Depression didn't especially depress me for quite a while, actually. I didn't notice it until after it had ended, and the economy boomed during World War Two.

PLACE: The Hospital, located in The Little Town Nearby, a burg of about 12,000 God-fearing Christians, two Jews, and five atheists. Nuns operated this hospital and advised pregnant women on how to cope.

Consider that Step One for every living entity is to preserve its power. From a paramecium to Julius Caesar, an organism first of all seeks to retain whatever influence it has.

Step Two consists of exercising said power. If you've captured Gaul go ahead and invade England. And then where's Scotland? Who are those guys in drag? And what are those Jupiter-awful sounds they make that stampede our horses?

Step Three involves expanding or enlarging this power. Well, Adolf, the western front is going pretty well; let's invade Russia. It doesn't always work out.

From plants to one-celled beasties raging across a microscope slide to pussycats to politicians, we all follow that same pattern. We're hard-wired to do just that. And if a kid grows up on a small farm and attends a school a mile away, he will strive desperately to get to town as often as possible, because people had fun there. And when he wears out that town, he'll seek out a larger one. Seeking what? A larger microscope slide? Perhaps an even larger burg to visit now and then? I seemed to have leanings that way.

After I became a teacher, I would describe to students The Given Circumstances of my youth; many of them blinked and gawked at me as though I had just arrived from another planet, which in a way I had. I grew up on that family farm during the Great Depression and World War Two in pleasant if peasant-like conditions, before the Rural Electrification Act; no electricity, no gas, no running water.

After World War Two the Rural Electrification Act wired us all up to 110-volt alternating current. That was a good thing to do. It was a good thing, and our government did it. It can happen.

Although I knew next to nothing about the outside world, I soon developed an interest in and a craving for more information. I hankered for a wider range of experience. I had an itch for a piece of the action, wherever and whatever it was. But before I could change my situation I had to understand it, so I began inspecting and questioning my little world. I needed to step into a wider perspective to begin that analysis, but I couldn't find a place to stand. Archimedes had the same problem, they tell me. A Greek guy, way back. I don't think he ever found a place.

But no one told me anything helpful, and there seemed to be a plan to keep me as ignorant as possible for as long as possible. I resented that, but it seemed the way of country folk. I thought it desirable, even necessary, to overcome that and leave it behind. As I grew older, though, I noticed that country folk were intimidated by city ways. This led them to make sharp distinctions between "city people" and "farm people," and especially between city kids and farm kids. When The Mother called my son a city kid, it was not a term of admiration or endearment. But he didn't know that, and I didn't tell him till much later.

The Geezer Disease, Genealogy

My family history begins with The Father. He didn't own the little farm we inhabited; he rented it from a Depression-era Miss Daisy complete with Cadillac and chauffeur. The Father's side of the family came to America from Ireland in the early eighteenth century, first to Pennsylvania, then to Ohio, cutting their roads through the forests.

In his youth, The Father worked on a pipeline gang laying a gas pipe from Oklahoma across the Mississippi River into Illinois. He must have paid attention in school since he could read, write, and cipher, so he kept the account books for the gang and bought the food for the men who dug ditches all day. They got hungry, digging a ditch from Oklahoma to Illinois.

As they say in the movies, jump cut:

The Mother's grandfather (we called him Original Joe) immigrated to the Midwest from Bohemia about 1853, and he bought a small farm near a Bohemian settlement not far from a metropolis. One of Original Joe's sons, The Grandfather, later took charge of the farm, then sold it and moved a few miles to the outskirts of a trifling little town nearby. The Mother grew up there and began clerking in a general store to which she walked six days a week.

Apparently, she paid attention in school, too; her employers regarded her highly. One day as she busily clerked away in strode a handsome young Irishman to buy food for his pipeline gang. You might have heard the distant rumble of thunder, and the young Irishman later became The Father.

After a three-year courtship they married and moved to Montana, where one of The Father's brothers operated a wretched little grocery store. The Mother being an experienced clerk and The Father being handy at whatever needed doing, the arrangement worked out well.

When this building was a general store The Father met The Mother here while buying food for his ditch-diggers. It's a funeral home now, but I don't know what that means. Photograph by the author.

But as rational people they could not endure Montana winters. Winter gets pretty chilly in the Midwest, but Montana winters can get so cold that if you throw a bucket of water up in the air it will freeze before it hits the ground. Those states up there get metaphysically cold.

ASIDE: I told a friend about this kind of cold once, and he proclaimed me a lying son-of-a-bitch to one and all. I refer any doubters to Google and the Internet for confirmation. Or you can just wait for a cold snap and try it yourself.

The Mother became The Mother when her first child, a girl, arrived, and soon after that the three of them fled down south and rented a farm, The Little House on the Prairie, Part One. No trace of it remains, but people described it as a miserable excuse for a house on an equally miserable plot of earth. They made do there for a while, and then a boy child happened in 1922. Eventually the family upgraded to The Little House on the Prairie, Part Two, into which they installed me in 1934.

Some of our relatives found the place acceptable enough to come and visit or even settle close by. The Mother's older sister, The Aunt, a placid soul, and her husband, The Swede, moved to a farm about a mile or so away from The Parents' farm. The two sisters in turn attracted their parents, The Grandfather and Grandmother.

The Grandfather was a woodsman of note and a pleasant sort to have around. People who knew him, though, suggested he might have been a few twists short of a Slinky. For example, he kept loose pipe tobacco and .22 bullets in the same pocket and at least once stuffed a shell into his pipe bowl. Lighting the tobacco caused no trouble, but a bit later the pipe bowl exploded, leaving only the stem in his mouth. I only heard about this; I didn't see it. I hope it happened. If a story gets told enough times, it did happen.

The Grandmother, on the other hand, everyone considered as nutty as a peach-orchard boar. She came to stay at our house once; she had a habit of traveling from one child's house to another, then moving on after the fighting broke out. Shortly after arriving at our place she began to line out The Mother, telling her how to run her household. Such a ploy might have worked elsewhere, but The Father took The Grandmother aside and did a little lining out of his own. Things returned to normal.

The Grandmother also didn't do well with little kiddies. Once The Parents took The Sister and me to The Father's hometown in Ohio for a few weeks. They left The Grandmother to tend to things and The Brother to do the milking and chores.

While The Grandmother just wallowed in that old-time religion The Brother did not. Nor did The Father. Nor did, in the fullness of time, I.

The Brother managed to get onto the roof one sunny day while The Grandmother washed dishes, and he used a hand mirror to flash a light around the kitchen, pretty much freaking her out. She thought she was having a visitation from her Creator or her guardian angel, possibly both.

ASIDE: For those of you not raised in this tradition, your Creator supposedly assigned an angel to watch over every baby when it was born. Some angels had it pretty easy, but they said mine went AWOL about 1945.

The Brother didn't fess up for about five decades, by which time the statute of limitations had run out and The Grandmother had gone on to aggravate God.

The Grandmother's nadir in family relations came the day The Uncle died of a heart attack. One Sunday during the War we went to their place for dinner; The Father took along a bottle of bourbon The Brother had sent them. We lived in a dry state during the war, and hard liquor was almost impossible to find, although bootleggers weren't. And a bordering state was wet. I didn't partake, yet.

A massive heart attack felled The Uncle just as we drove onto their place. Much confusion and uproar; we all loved that man. A few days later The Father remembered the bourbon and started looking for it. I remember his comment, "Why, God damn it, Grandma stole the whiskey!" I thought about making that the title of this book, but people advised me not to.

The Sibs

So I came to the farm to live with, besides The Mother and The Father, my two siblings, older than me by sixteen and twelve years. The Sister had desperately wanted a little sister; she sobbed for days after the word came to her that I had turned out male; they had referred to me in the embryonic stage as Margaret. I don't think The Sister looked at my face for about a week.

In due course The Sister graduated from high school. The Father told her that he didn't believe in sending girls to college; they just got married and had kids. She became a secretary for a few years, then she got married and had kids. While she dated the man she would later marry, I extorted him out of all manner of cap pistols, fireworks, chocolate goodies, and other treasures. He joined those who thought I was spoiled rotten, soon enough. But I suddenly had serious competition for The Spoiled Sweepstakes; The Sister and her mate began reproducing, accumulating four girl-children. As The Brother said of The Sister's husband, "That man just doesn't have any boy bugs in him!"

The Brother, on the other hand, quickly became an idol for me, as older brothers often do. He was my only brother, and I told him once I never wanted another.

The Brother had many appealing talents; he could just do lots of stuff. He once talked one of his grade school buddies into sticking wooden matches in his hatband, then The Brother lit them by grazing the match tips with .22 rifle bullets fired from a short distance. The Parents caught him and took him aside and spoke to him. They spoke to him some more when they saw him bulldogging jackrabbits, because those speedy little beasts would duck under barbed wire fences, which spoiled the game altogether.

He could ride spectacularly well on one of the fastest horses in the county, bareback, sometimes indeed standing up on the horse's back, which attracted attention. He made good grades in school, although he often grew bored. This ennui once led him to accidentally blow up the school stove. He meant no harm, true, but the singed teacher took small comfort in that. Once more The Brother was taken aside and spoken to.

I didn't just want to be like him, I wanted to be him. The Brother was a chemist; I studied chemistry. He played billiards well; I pursued the game. He liked poker; I took it up in depth. Eventually I began meandering off on my own, but that's another chapter. The Brother even willingly helped with the chores around the farm, and that's when we came to a fork in the road, and I took it. Chemistry, at which The Brother excelled, lost its appeal, and I began to find my own way. I wonder if sometimes The Father didn't wonder how he happened to sire a chemist and a theatre professor.

The Sister, on the other hand, loved farms and farming.

Little House on the Prairie, Part Two

So that constitutes Scene One. Our lack of modern utilities back then dumbfounds young people today. For my first ten years we used coal oil lanterns for light, a well for water, and wood for fuel. Eventually we obtained electricity, water lines, and gas heating. Even an air conditioner, in the fullness of time.

I was quite a bit younger than The Sibs. Some authorities contend that the youngest child gets spoiled; my siblings would rush down to the footlights to throw roses and applaud that premise. I became spoiled rotten. Legend has it that at lunch once I demanded a dill pickle, a delicacy The Mother created with Bohemian inspiration. For some reason she refused to give me one, so I crawled under the table, announcing to one and all I would remain there until the pickle arrived. Yes, they took me aside and spoke to me.

But consider this: I got my pickle.

I vaguely recall other rites of passage, for example, my first haircut. I should say my first commercial haircut because The Mother had been scalping me regularly for several years. For whatever reason they hauled me into The Little Town Nearby and delivered me to a sure-enough stand-up barber.

Back then when little nippers appeared in barbershops the barber put a padded plank across the chair arms and deposited the tot on the plank, raising his head to a workable height. After he quit cutting hair the barber doused the kid's head with a putrid cologne and sent him on his way.

I hated the whole idea; I felt helpless in the hands of this stranger and his cutlery, so I raised unmitigated hell through the entire operation, but to no avail. The barber promised me a lollypop if I cooled it, so I did. When he got done it looked like he had painted my hair on me. For that matter, it smelled like it, too.

I could and would wail mighty wails if occasion demanded it and I thought I might profit thereby. Take for example, The Little Town Nearby and its grocery store, Safeway's, a company still in existence.

The clerks would bag up our groceries for us to tote home. The clerk packed up our goods one evening, using a paper bag. This particular swine, trying for style and élan, snapped the bag open. One night he nailed me right in the eye, causing pain, leading me into a sobbing fit. The pain went away after a while, but the indignity of it all disgusted me, so I cried myself to sleep. Of course, that didn't do me a bit of good.

I came to realize it was a lost cause and that crying fits would do me no good whatsoever in the great scheme of things. I tried it a time or two more, even after The Mother started hauling me off to church, but soon gave it up.

Ways I Found to Hurt Myself

I didn't need to go to town to get hurt. Farms in those days offered many means for self-mutilation. Lots of pointy cutting tools and big heavy iron things and large animals could damage a small boy if he was prone to dreaming, as I was.

For example, I once stood on a concrete platform holding a plowshare. I have no idea what plan I had for that plowshare, and even less idea why I dropped it, point first, onto by left big toe. But I did. They say I raced to the house holding my left foot up in the air. I don't remember it quite like that.

The Mother brewed up a small tub of hot water and Epsom salts and rammed my foot into it; the pain eventually abated. But my toe swelled up and the nail turned utterly black before falling off, new growth replacing it. I did considerable wailing over that episode.

Probably my most serious hurting took place in our barn while I watched The Brother rearrange loose hay in the haymow. While he forked it from one pile to another, I gamboled about nearby. The barn-builders had put three-foot square holes in the upper floor to facilitate getting hay from above into the stalls below. I played too close to one of them, though The Brother warned me to take care or I'd fall through and bust myself. I continued cavorting around, of course, until I slid off the hay and sizzled down through one of the holes. He turned out to be utterly correct.

The barn at The Little House on the Prairie, Part Two. Adolescent vandals from The Little Town Nearby burned it down after we had moved to another place. Photo by the author.

I went whistling down eight or ten feet, then my chin smashed into the grain box on the end of the stall, knocking me colder than the proverbial wedge; I still have the scar. I don't remember much after that, but The Brother pulled me out of the stall and carried me up to the house. The Mother saw him coming and screamed, "Oh, he's dead! I know he's dead." I lived, but I didn't respond to their ministrations, so once again they lugged me into The Little Town Nearby and gave me over to our kindly old family physician. We had no such thing as Emergency Rooms back then, but if you appeared spurting blood at an M.D.'s office you could expect immediate attention. I often wonder what would happen if one showed up at a physician's office with a bleeding wound. I expect they'd fix it.

I didn't cry during this episode, being unconscious. The M.D. took a stitch or two in my chin and sent me forth to find more trouble.

Another time The Father assigned The Brother to sack up some grain in order to transport it somewhere. When I passed by him on some errand of mischief, he put me to work holding the feed sack open so he could scoop grain into it. No problem, until I grew bored and wanted to know if the sack wasn't about filled, so I stuck my head down to see, but that lacked good judgment. The Brother had a shovel full of grain headed toward the sack, so the front edge of the shovel clipped off about a third of one of my front teeth. It cut my lip, too, and I bled a whole bunch.

I don't recall that they took me to town for that one. My front upper teeth had grown in crooked anyway, and I kept my upper lip covering them most of the time. I didn't much want to go into town; I craved desperately to stay out of the clutches of The Dentist. He powered his drill with a foot peddle, like sewing machines in those days. The bit heated up almost immediately, and I wondered if the results didn't forecast the pains of Hell for my sins, real or imaginary, past, present, and future.

That same dentist later found a remedy for my crooked teeth; he took them out. A memorable operation, that, involving considerable hurt, but by then I had grown too butch to cry. He replaced them with an enormously bothersome partial bridge that cost one hundred dollars. There you go; nowadays you can't get a dentist to let you in the door for a hundred dollars. I still have a bridge up front, but now it's a permanent one.

The farm was overrun with dangerous devices, such as pitchforks or hay hooks that had fallen down and marinated for a few decades in assorted manures. When a barefoot boy like me stepped on it a prong punctured him, injecting typhoid and God knows what other types of germs deep into his foot. This would involve another trip to the M.D., who gave you a shot that hurt more than the pitchfork. But it saved me from typhus, or so they told me.

What it boils down to is that farms were dangerous places, not just for kids. Full-grown men killed themselves with tractors from time to time. If a bull got upset about something, he might gore the source of his discontent. Women might have explosions in their kitchens, or accidentally poison members of their family. No doubt about it, we all had to keep alert at all times. Of course, telling a country kid to keep alert was about as effective as trying to teach your farm dog to fart "The Flight of the Bumble Bee," but The Parents tried. Sure, they tried, but without much success.

Rural Hygiene

Matters of personal hygiene began with a literal outhouse, located about thirty feet from the back door of the house.

We had a neighbor lady, a widow, who had a window put in her outhouse door so she could sit and watch traffic go by. Different strokes for different folks. Or as the French say, *c'est le maniere different pour les gens different.*

We had to move our outhouse every few years, a hideous, Sisyphean task that involved digging a new pit, dragging the outhouse over the new excavation, usually with horses, then covering up the old hole, like a cat. On a blistering summer day that job would make a small boy fantasize about other ways to live. Flies the size of middle infielders circled around us while we finished the job. Later the flies came inside and joined us for lunch.

I once read for every human being on earth there are seventeen million flies. I don't doubt that a bit, but we had a few million more than our share. Lots of stuff on our farm attracted flies, and try as we might, we couldn't keep them all out with screen doors or windows.

The outhouse at The Little House on the Prairie, Part Three. I converted it into a chemical laboratory when we installed an indoor facility. My lab was small, but pungent. Photograph by the author.

Most of the country folk also used the expedient chamber pot, kept under the bed. Jocularly termed the "thunder jug," the more fastidious had a lid to put on it till dawn when its contents could be heaved outside, perhaps onto a cat or bunny or something.

Laundry piled up, and The Mother dealt with it, but without modern washers or dryers. She concocted a primitive soap from lye and animal fat. Some said it could take the chrome off a Buick bumper, but it did the job on dirty clothes. The stores in The Little Town Nearby also sold some early detergents.

Early clothing washing equipment. The Mother washed clothes in one tub, rinsed them, and then ran them through the rollers into the other tub. Better than a river and a flat rock. Courtesy of the Cowley County Kansas Historical Museum.

One of my nieces got her arm caught between two rollers once; I found that altogether droll, but the grownups seemed alarmed. The niece bellowed like a baby bull, but she wasn't hurt. She'd pretty quickly taken over the crying jags after I'd given them up.

To dry the clothing, The Father erected a clothesline just behind the house. The Mother pinned the various wet cloth things to the metal wires, and in a hot summer wind they dried very quickly indeed, the humidity dipping to single digits. We usually had a hell of a high wind, too.

If our clothes got dirty, so did we, so bathing constituted another hygienic problem. A pitcher, a bowl, and a bar of homemade lye soap took care of day-to-day ministrations, but when it came time for a sit-down, full-bore bath, a galvanized tub appeared. I recall vividly splashing around in it one Saturday afternoon, getting scoured down, when The Uncle and The Aunt appeared at the kitchen door with a shiny red tricycle for me, thus fulfilling a dream I had since I first discovered such things existed.

I whooped for joy, leaped out of the tub, straddled the trike in all my naked glory, and vanished, a blurred comet of pink and scarlet. I refused to be caught or otherwise interfered with until my legs gave out and I toddled home. The shame of it all overcame The Mother; The Father and The Uncle roared with delight, and The Aunt beamed her iconic placid beam. That trike was my first transportation device, until I got a horse.

Trash

We generated trash of all sorts, just as any properly run household does. We had to deal with it ourselves; there was no garbage pickup out in the country. We didn't have as much as you might think. Leftover foodstuffs we recycled for the animals; hogs got slop, for example, and welcome to it. Pets came in for their share, too. I considered chicken livers just one step above manure, but our cats loved them.

For other stuff we used a small bluff behind the chicken house and converted it into a dump; there we could discard broken things, worn out tools, and unneeded debris of all sorts. It wasn't a large pile of stuff; during the Depression people made do and used things over and over. The Mother kept saying that centuries in the future archeologists would decide there had been an iron mine there, from all the rust and metallic ruins they would find. The Father lost a pocketknife annually, simplifying Christmas for me; I think I gave him about ten of them, one a year.

I visited that site a few years ago; our castoffs continue to merge into the soil. I didn't find anything worth rescuing, though.

Winters

Sometimes the weather supplied big-time distractions. We'd have snow from time to time, even heavy snow, much fun in which to play. To use the outdoor privy a kid needed heavy bundling before he could get out of the house after a snow. I spent inordinate amounts of time getting the thirty feet to and from the facility, but you get nothing for nothing—that seat got mighty cold in sub-zero weather.

Once rain fell and immediately froze, which left everything coated with about a half inch of ice. Nothing much moved in such conditions, but I wheedled my way outside and dug out my sled. A sloping lane led from a road down to our house and barn, perhaps a hundred yards. Gravel covered this lane, but the ice had formed on top of the pebbles, and I assumed I could have a phenomenal sled ride down the lane to the barn, and indeed I did. Zip-ah-dee-doo-dah.

As usual, my plan contained flaws. I underestimated my speed when I reached the area between the house and barn, and I had no idea how to stop my sled or even slow it down. But I could steer the sled a little bit, and an open gate led to a bottomland field near our creek. That gave me another fifty yards in which to reconsider my immediate future and what chances I might have for survival.

But that bottomland had cattle in it that day, and a bossy had meandered over toward the gate, broadside to me. I made some quick choices—I didn't want to hit the cow for a number of reasons; it might bust me up, and it wouldn't do her any good, either. By dragging one foot on the ice I missed her, though, and started figuring out how to stop. The bottomland had a woven wire fence around it, so I managed a sideways slide to miss the fence posts and hit the fence, which flexed enough to stop the sled without killing me. I did no more sledding that day. Or ever again. But that cow remained kind of nervous and twitchy for a few years whenever I got near her.

Let's Twist Again

We lived in Tornado Alley, so we had twisters to amuse us from time to time.

During thunderstorms we sometimes saw tornadoes dancing around on the horizon. At night we had no real information about how big, how bad, or exactly where they were. Weathermen had pretty crude technology in those days, so if they happened, they happened. The radio gave us some data as to location, but during nights illuminated only by lightning, people often reported telephone poles as killer tornadoes. They still do.

If the storms got bad enough, we trooped off to the storm cellar, which doubled as a storage site for canned food, centipedes, snakes, and big wooly spiders. We usually took a kerosene light along with us.

Once during a storm The Father decided he had to know if the wind had destroyed his farm, so he braced himself and opened the door a few inches. The wind caught the door and flipped him out into the yard a few feet away, and we had a hell of a time getting the door closed again. I found that more than slightly amusing, but I decided not to laugh about it.

The storm cellar to which we fled during tornado weather. In our time the door was made of wood, but the concrete roof was the same. Photo by the author.

A little bitty tornado had passed between the barn and the house, tearing up a hay wagon and reducing a small shed to rubbish, but doing no catastrophic damage, like destroying our house or barn.

Tornadoes still frighten me, though. Seventy years later if I see one or hear one coming I'll find a hole and get in it. If I can't find a hole, I'll dig one. Shovels help, but I don't absolutely have to have one. I would try to make do with four sets of nails and my teeth, if it came to that. I did once look up into a tornado funnel as it crossed over The Little Town Nearby. That experience made me a born-again, temporary Christian for several days.

While small tornadoes seemed sort of cute and pet-like, every so often a monster hit and ended the fun. One night in May, 1955, some nineteen tornadoes hit the Midwest, killing about a hundred people. A small town about fifteen miles from The Little Town Nearby suffered massive damage; seventy-seven people killed out of a population of five hundred, with almost no buildings left intact. The National Guard deployed, as did all disaster agencies, and eventually that little town rose again, and it prospers to this day. But the citizens now have storm cellars that are state of the art.

A day or two after the tornado trashed that little town a caravan of Mennonites in horse-drawn wagons appeared, a sect I had only heard of, but I thought they had cornered the market on silliness. They brought tools with them and asked if they could help. The survivors assured them they could. They camped and toiled until they had finished the job. Other religions had prayer meetings. I noted with some interest who seemed to be the most helpful to the survivors. I didn't see fit to discuss this distinction with anyone, though.

Of course, in The Little Town Nearby the citizens felt secure, telling one another what an old Indian had told the early settlers–they need not fear tornados because their land lay between two rivers, and tornados couldn't cross water. I doubt the old Indian had ever seen a waterspout, for indeed a tornado will cross water, pick up a creek, and dump it nearby. I met an old farmer once who lived near a trifling town, and a tornado went across his creek, sucked it dry, and then dumped it on his porch, flushing the old farmer off into his driveway.

Old Indians can be just as full of complete and utter nonsense as all the rest of us.

Disgusting Dust

I considered all the dust on a farm pretty off-putting. My older relatives remembered the Dust Bowl of the 1930s, but I wasn't aware of that disaster. Still, the wind blows a lot in the Midwest, and it moves all the available dust. A south wind blew red dust up from the south, and a north wind blew it back again. West winds had been the biggies during the Dust Bowl. I don't remember any east winds.

Unless we sealed our windows and doors hermetically tight the dust came in around the frames. Indeed, snow did the same thing; I awoke many a morning with a dusting of snow on my blankets. Stepping out of bed onto a linoleum-covered floor would cause a small boy to prance like a champion.

Since automobiles then had no air conditioning, we rode around with the windows down, and dust kicked up by the car found its way inside. After a year or so the felt lining in the top of the car became saturated with dust, dust that fell out of the lining when the car hit a bump. I hated that. We had to drive two and one-half miles to the nearest highway, which then led us another two miles to The Little Town Nearby. So we had plenty of bumps and ruts to negotiate, and we would get showered with falling grit and dust as we sped along.

Racism

I had an aunt, two of them, actually, who loudly and frequently proclaimed any dark-skinned person as inferior, both socially and physically. And morally, God knows. How they came up with this concept, I have no idea, but I suspect The Grandmother.

One aunt struck me as particularly obnoxious. She started with African-Americans, of course, but then included Mexicans, Italians, and Greeks. That's the way she had been raised, as had most of the people she knew.

That aunt's point on Mexicans hit home because our church in The Little Town Nearby had a Mexican couple among its parishioners. They sat in the back and took Communion last. And in the church cemetery Mexicans had their plot segregated into one small section. The older I got the more I saw all this as hypocritical. I mean we had a prayer, a very popular one, that usually started "Our Father. . . ." The Little Town Nearby had had an active Klan membership in the 1930s, and while it didn't take root and flourish it took some getting over. The Father assured me that "niggers didn't mind being called niggers; if you called one he would come over to see what you wanted." I felt sure The Father, one of the fairest men I ever met, erred on this point, but again I kept my trap shut. It would have done no one any good had I tried to correct him.

When I started working and bought a television set for The Parents, I read once that one of our two and one-half channels would feature Louis Armstrong. One afternoon I assured The Mother that she'd never heard anything like his trumpet and led her into the living room to see him. When Satchmo come on stage she exclaimed, "Why, it's a nigger!" and that ended that. I knew damned well she was wrong, very wrong, and unlearning racism became a major goal of my young life.

I remember later being in The Pool Hall downtown, listening to the elders discussing a heavyweight championship fight to be held that evening. Joe Louis, a black man, was to defend his title against a white challenger. One of the locals asked a black janitor how he thought the fight would go.

The janitor paused, thought a moment, and then drawled, "Oh, I suppose they'll give to Joe."

I repeat, "Oh, I suppose they'll give it to Joe."

What a masterpiece of evasion! How carefully thought out a reply! Richard Pryor or Flip Wilson would have had different responses. So would have Malcolm X. I imagine that janitor had a lot of experience at being black in the 1950s in mid-America, so he didn't think anything, he just supposed. Black people didn't share their opinions with whitey back then.

The "Amos 'n' Andy" radio show also underscored our prejudices. To his eternal credit, The Brother explained to me the long-term effects of African sun, and since my parents supported racism, I took an opposing stand. I didn't so much consider myself moral as uppity. Reading Mark Twain did me a world of good, and a lot later I read and watched *Roots*. Applause, applause! In fact, I just ordered the entire series so I could watch it again. Once in a while something comes along that almost justifies television. *Lonesome Dove. Deadwood.*

ASIDE: I had a relative who hated pretty much everyone, but blacks especially. He told me he craved to see some white boy go up against Louis, cut him to ribbons for ten rounds, then put him away. That was typical thinking for those days. Lots of people wanted to see "A Great White Hope." I don't think the Broadway show or the movie did them much good.

I'd been brought up in the racist tradition, but the mythology about black people's inferiority just didn't hold up under examination. In high school I met many black kids; some were dumb as stumps; some were mighty sharp. The same was true of Mexicans. They seemed to be just like other people, after all. The defense rests. At least I couldn't tell much difference after I got past pigmentation, even if my supposedly older and wiser kin and neighbors mostly could. And did. I began to realize maybe I was right and they were wrong. But I kept still about it. For then. Later I felt free to share the benefits of my experience with anyone handy, but back then I kept mum.

So there we have it; warts and all. I wanted to go elsewhere to seek fulfillment, but that was a long time coming. In the meantime I pursued diversions where I could, and I took it one day at a time. But then there isn't really any other way, is there?

CHAPTER TWO

DIVERSIONS, SUCH AS THEY WERE, OR, FUN ON THE FARM

I grew up—well, taller—seeking diversions. I wasn't doing anything from which I needed diversion, really, but I sought wider horizons. Everyone does. Kids actually think they can pull it off. And once in a great while they do manage it. I didn't know what sort of odds I was up against, but I'd have tried for it anyway, had anyone given me a clue about it. Of course, no one did, not The Parents, not The One-Room Country School I attended later, and not the Church. Nada. No one. Makes you wonder just why they didn't, doesn't it?

Going to Town

The Little Town Nearby offered much more amusement than the farm. I tagged along with The Father when he took jobs to the blacksmith, for example. Local farmers called the blacksmith a horse, not because he was, but to describe his gladiatorial muscularity.

The Little Town Nearby boasted a train station. Train tracks ran out into the country, but we rarely saw any traffic out there. Steam engines pulled freight, mainly coal, which they still do, only now they use diesel. Folks attending the County Fair, seated in the grandstand, would often see trains passing through town, bleating out warnings as the came to crossings. A long train could stop traffic on a main highway for a half hour or so. And there just wasn't a damned thing you could do about it.

A Streamliner such as passed through The Little Town Nearby twice a day. It stimulated dreams of escape for me, to a world beyond my reach or imagination. From the author's collection.

But in the evenings—I want to say about nine o'clock, since I got to stay up late—a Streamliner, a passenger train, made a stop at the station. They had an honest-to-God sit-down dining car. We could gawk in like the rubes we were and see folks lounging at tables drinking and eating and looking bored with travel, just as any experienced voyager should. I envied the hell out of them and hoped someday I could have a meal on a passenger train. Of course, I hadn't tasted any of that food at that time; I had a lot to learn.

The Father also took me along to the cattle sales rink on Saturday afternoon at the county fairgrounds. (The Little Town Nearby boasted the rank of County Seat.) The farmers sat in steeply tiered seats on three sides of a rink, into which the staff led the beasts. An auctioneer described them, the audience bid on or rejected them, and the staff led the brutes away. I don't recall The Father ever buying or selling anything, but he must have done so. I wondered then why auctioneers used that strange rhythmic chant; years later, I still wonder. But these trips offered a change of pace, no matter that The Father's hopes of turning a son into a farmer crashed and burned yet again.

A couple of times parts of The Little Town Nearby flooded since no one had yet erected dikes. A nearby small river would expand to a half-mile width, and The Father would go in and have a look at the flood. Luckily, he took me along. As we watched the waters invade the town and destroy houses, he told me that anyone who lived in an area that had ever been flooded qualified as a damned fool. I agreed heartily, and I still do. And I've not been flooded, nor will I be.

Murders of Crows

Well, amusements come and amusements go, but one diversion never paled for me: hunting crows. I had once somehow amassed ten dollars, and my brother approached me, offering a deal: a single shot Remington .22 rifle for the ten, no questions asked. It still seems like a good idea at the time. I think The Brother had a date and needed a few bucks. Some female never knew how much I did for her.

I had for some years owned a Red Ryder BB gun, a lovely toy, admittedly dangerous. I laid waste to the sparrow population with it, and occasionally shot a bullet through a chicken's tail feathers, just to turn her around. I was hoping to screw one into the ground, but I never could.

I made a few shekels with that BB gun. The Mother opined that sparrows brought mites into the chicken house, reducing productivity, and therefore offered me a bounty on "spatzies," as we called them. Perhaps a nickel a corpse; I don't remember. I would submit the dead birds to her; she'd pay up, then hurl them over the bluff into the trash heap to decay with the rest of the bluff stuff.

After I'd thinned out the local flocks it came to me to recycle some of the feathered bodies, but rigor mortis had set in and The Mother detected my greedy little scam and shut down the operation, once and for all. She also took me aside and spoke to me, one more time.

The Brother's .22 rifle, however, extended my range. I shot tin cans, bottles, and small game before my trigger-happy eye noticed crows, widely considered pests by the farmers. They cawed out for elimination.

A crowd of crows is called a murder of crows, they tell me. I didn't know that, but I tried to murder as many crows as I possibly could. True, they outnumbered me, and they seemed somehow to know the effective range of a .22 rifle bullet and stayed just beyond it. But I found places to hide and waited them out. I opened up a new avenue of warfare by gouging a hole in our wooden silo so I could lurk within and shoot through the hole. They eventually figured that out, being amazingly smart birds.

I didn't even dent the crow population; they still prosper in that area.

ASIDE: I recently read an article about the smartest animals: elephants, dolphins, dogs, and such. Crows made the list as the only birds, which made me feel better.

Would I shoot a crow now? I don't really know, but if it showed up in the grocery store and tried to take my food away from me, I expect I would.

Nowadays we might find more humane methods for keeping the pests under control; in those days we didn't. If you've ever seen what a murder of crows can do to a patch of corn intended to become roasting ears or popcorn, you might understand our agricultural morality back then. In a larger sense, we were fighting for our lives, or more specifically, our food. The Father won most of the fights; some of our neighbors won the battles; some lost, held farm sales to convert everything into cash, then moved to town for some other kind of work. When a crayon factory opened in The Little Town Nearby, a lot of the workers were failed farmers. Other options included the County Poor Farm, which was a sort of retreat home for farm families who just couldn't cut it. It's not there anymore, but I don't know what happened to it. I wonder if some government agency at some level took over its functions.

Slipping the Surly Bonds

My outstanding achievement from those days happened late in my career as a squat-low. I listened faithfully to "Jack Armstrong, the All-American Boy," a quarter-hour radio serial sponsored by Wheaties, the Breakfast of Champions, sort of a cereal serial. I even ate Wheaties to support Jack and his adventures. Then the sponsors ran a contest and made me an offer I couldn't refuse. We kiddy contestants had to name a Piper Cub airplane, a small yellow plane seating two people, rather like a flying Model T. They resulted from a company titled Piper, and their model name was Cub.

A Piper Cub in flight. Most were painted yellow. Sometimes the door fell open. Seat belts were mandatory. From the author's collection.

I had to send in a Wheaties box top and a dime with my name for the Cub. Most of the kiddy radio programs offered similar scams; Tom Mix hustled a ring that enabled you to see behind yourself, but no one ever appeared there. Captain Midnight offered a decoder badge, which I still have. True, I haven't received many coded messages lately, but I'm ready for them if and when the call comes. But I don't think Captain Midnight is on the radio any more. Pity.

First prize in the Jack Armstrong contest? An honest-to-God Piper Cub. In my wildest fantasies I couldn't imagine owning a Cub; for one thing, where would I have kept it? What did it eat? Consider that most of us had never seen an airplane and had certainly never flown in one. I don't think we even knew anyone who had flown. Maybe some distant relatives. Most of us hadn't yet had a train ride, even.

I pondered quite a while about a possible name. Finally, I decided to give it my best shot: "Gremlins' Gripe." OK, it doesn't like, sing, or anything, but at age ten I hadn't yet read *Hamlet* or *Huckleberry Finn.* I suppose if I'd sent in "a consummation devoutly to be wish'd" or "whoopjambareehoo" someone in authority would have taken me aside and spoken to me.

Time passed, and I mostly forgot about the whole thing. Then the mailman brought an envelope for me, immediately putting The Mother at Def Con One, and the letter inside said that I had in fact won—not the Piper Cub itself, but a thirty-minute ride in one, about twenty-fifth prize or so. If I took the letter and certificate to the nearest airport, they would fly me around a half hour at no charge. Entering the contest turned out to be a masterstroke that befuddled The Parental Units to the max. Winning a prize in such a contest shocked them even more.

The Father decided to resolve the matter, so he drove me to the local airfield, a pasture with a hangar at one end. A few light planes stayed there, and The Father confronted the guy who ran the place. He agreed to the validity of the whole thing and asked when we wanted to perform this astonishment. We set a day and time, and I tried to sleep nights.

Eventually the day arrived, as days sometimes do. The Parents stopped to pick up My Best Friend, then off we went to the airfield. The pilot queried me with some vigor about whether or not I suffered from motion sickness, which I didn't, so he put me in the back seat and took off. We rolled along the runway and became airborne.

Well, there's no time like the first time, is there? I stared down at The Little Town Nearby as we circled around at perhaps a thousand feet. The pilot gave thanks I didn't deposit my breakfast down his back. I had a camera with me, but I forgot to take any photos. Then I remembered I lived on a farm and asked the pilot if he could fly over it. He did, and I finally took a picture. One. One photograph during a half hour flight. Can we say nervous? As The Rancher (you'll meet him later) would say, "Nervous as a virgin on the verge."

Our farm from the air, the only photo I took during my plane ride. The house, barn, and outbuildings are grouped left center. This is Little House on the Prairie, Part Three. Photo by the author.

We landed without incident, taxied up to the hangar, and deplaned. Thrilled doesn't begin to explain how I felt, but I stayed cool. At least as cool as I could be with every nerve and muscle quivering like the strings on a bull fiddle.

The Father wanted to know if I had been scared or sick. The Mother tried for years to figure out how I'd pulled off this outrage. The Best Friend progressed far beyond green with envy, he went off the visible light spectrum altogether. In a metaphorical sense, I had seen the elephant, as they used to say at the circus.

When I returned to The Country Grade School, of course, I no longer associated with the masses; I had become The Boy Who Had Flown. I lived now in a world distinct from that of my grubby little companions.

The Teacher avoided the subject; she too suffered from envy. Older boys pretended they hadn't heard about it. But I had a witness. And a photo. Tom Sawyer running off to be a pirate was just a mouse fart when compared to a kid winning a flight around The Little Town Nearby. On a clear day I might look wistfully into the skies, a slight smile on my lips, and the girls just knew I was reliving My Flight.

"Gremlins' Gripe" brought me my first payment as a writer, even if only two words, far better than some I've received since. More important, I had set new limits for shenaniganism. In later days we might say I had raised the bar for downright uppityness and outrageousness and giving The Parents new and exciting things to worry about.

The Metropolis

Another transcendental experience took place when The Brother returned from World War Two and the family planned a trip to The Metropolis—St. Louis—to visit relatives. I checked a map and discovered The Metropolis lay five hundred miles away—five hundred freakin' miles! The Little Town Nearby was only a five-mile trip; it would take a hundred times as long to get to The Metropolis. I hadn't been more than fifty miles away from home, and I had trouble conceiving such distances. I tried to estimate the distance to the Moon . . . a thousand miles, maybe? Two thousand? And what about the sun, which they told me was a star. The more I learned about them the more confused I became.

The Father didn't go; our cow-brutes had no relatives in The Metropolis, so he stayed home to run the farm. The Mother, The Aunt, The Brother, and I loaded up for the trek, all five hundred freakin' miles of it.

The Brother drove us on the two-lane highways of the day; no interstates existed then, at least not in the Midwest. The Metropolis seemed large, huge, probably because it contained about three million people. We went to the home of one of The Mother's sisters who had a large family of kids who all had first names beginning with the letter "J." That made no sense; still doesn't, but they did it that way. Not my problem.

However one of my problems manifested itself pretty quickly. After a few meals I felt a call of nature coming upon me. Now, I was used to outside one- and two-holers, but this house had plumbing and an indoor bathroom. I'd never used one; I'm not sure I had ever even seen one.

Pressures increased, so I finally approached The Brother, seeking procedural advice. To his eternal credit and my eternal appreciation, he calmly explained things and didn't make fun of me or tell anyone. The job done, the problem solved. I added another level of sophistication to my life.

Better things lay just ahead. As St. Louis residents still do, the family took their visiting relatives to the Zoo. The Zoo offered many wonders to a farm kid. Thanks to the World Book I knew about giraffes and gorillas, although they still impressed the hell out of me. I found it hysterical that the chimps would hurl their dung at their audience. I thought the orangutans personified cool, and I still do; I remembered them the first time I saw Dean Martin.

But the true wonders awaited me in the Reptile House. There I got to see real cobras, some of them spitting cobras, a nastiness I had not even imagined. Why, I wondered, why would a loving God inflict such a being on his other creatures? Serious doubts began to slither into my mind.

A python lying next to a log in one of the glassed cases stunned me. I studied it long and hard, then the full horror dawned on me: I had mistaken python for log. That dude could stretch out to about twenty feet and probably eat an entire Sunday school for a snack, prayer cards and all. And then polish off a nun or two for dessert.

The feared and dreaded Gaboon Viper. It gave me bad dreams for weeks after our confrontation. Luckily he was behind glass, and I was, too. Tough luck, Gaboon. From the author's collection.

I also got to see my first Gaboon Viper. Not a patch on the python for size, but I considered the name wonderful. I still do. Somewhat stocky for a snake, rather like the copperheads back home.

I wondered if a Gaboon Viper would chase a person if aroused; our copperheads sure would. I could out run them, of course, at least till I could find some weapon with which to dispatch said copperhead. And they came in pairs, the swine; if you killed one you could be sure another one lurked in the vicinity somewhere. When a farm kid learned this fact of life, he or she remained alert for several hours.

I once heard a fellow say on television that the Gaboon Viper got that name because it would come out and bite you on the gaboon. And then it would hang around and see how you liked it. I didn't believe that, but I became relieved when I learned the Gaboon Viper lived in Africa. I had no plans for a safari at that time, but if I had I'd have gone loaded for bear.

So I went back to grade school to show off my increased sophistication. I had now visited The Metropolis, seen the world, and knew everything. Or at least that's the way I acted, and most of the kids bought it.

This trip, like my Piper Cub escapade, further convinced me the world contained amusements and diversions to which I had no access while stuck on the farm. The obvious solution: get off the farm.

World War Two

On Sunday, the seventh of December, 1941, The Mother fetched me home from an early morning Mass. Around lunch the adults began listening to the radio and getting quite serious. I learned that the Japanese had bombed Pearl Harbor and we would fight a war with them. That war dominated our lives for the next four years and well beyond, indeed, to this day. Those good old days the older folks claimed to love so much came to a screeching halt when the first bombs fell. It ended when the bombs became atomic, wiping out eighty thousand enemies with one explosion.

The Brother graduated from the high school in The Little Town Nearby in 1940 and immediately enrolled at The Local College, a church-related, four-year institution, to study chemistry. This got him a draft dispensation, so he volunteered for the Navy in June 1944, probably the last man in the county to enlist. While he underwent boot camp near Chicago he sent me a sailor hat, which I wore daily to the huge envy of my classmates.

I remember The Parents seeing The Brother off when he finished Officer's Candidate School and prepared to ship out for the Pacific. They took him to the train station in The Little Town Nearby well in advance of his departure. But The Parents didn't wait to see him off; they left him there, which he mentioned some years later. The Sister insists that watching him leave, perhaps never to return, could have destroyed The Parents emotionally. For the first time in my life, I had to agree with her, but I never told her. It would have stunted her growth.

The Navy assigned him as gunnery officer to a Landing Ship Tank for the rest of the war. He thus experienced the invasion of Saipan, followed by a major typhoon. He said they never knew how hard the wind blew because it tore the anemometer off the ship

But one day he reappeared at the farm in uniform driving a late-model Chrysler New Yorker. He lived with us on The Little House on the Prairie, Part Three, for a while—I had to share a bed with him, and I don't know who suffered more—before he eventually moved to The Little Town Nearby.

World War Two colored everything, our thinking, the kids' games, and everyone's work. Most of the movies we saw concerned some aspect of war, and if a Saturday matinee began with "The Marine Hymn," a theatre full of small boys roared out their approval of organized murder and mayhem while blazing away with cap guns in all directions. We fabricated hand grenades out of half-chewed Jujubes and hurled them toward the screen when the foe appeared. I believe the ushers received extra compensation on Saturday afternoons.

This box contained playthings of mass destruction, considered a fitting present to celebrate Christ's birthday. From the author's collection.

War toys soon hit the market, for example a cardboard set of playthings, created by Built-Right and called Bild-A-Set. I got one for Christmas one year and the next year obtained a naval version of the same thing; ships, sailors, and I don't know what all. I was pretty miffed that it contained no Landing Ship Tanks, though, since The Brother went to war in one.

As the blurb proclaimed, 148 pieces of cardboard, cut out and ready to assemble, combined to make 39 complete units, soldiers and all manner of weapons. But they neglected to include any opponents. I needed some diminutive Japs or dwarf Nazis to blow up. I made do. The cats came in handy sometimes. Then, too, playing war, I could hide in an old barrel or discarded crate until a calf wandered by, then I would scream bloody murder and attack the beast. I rarely caught one, which was a good thing for both of us.

Gimme That Old Time Sex Education

Living on a farm means living with a lot of animals, obvious audio-visual aids for sex education. The male critters we hadn't castrated got it on from time to time with their appropriate females. We had bulls, of course, to service the cows and bring about calves, which we would sell or eat. The sequence seemed clear; bovine sex resulted in little bovines. Some primitive tribes cannot connect the two events, but I was hip enough to figure it out in a sort of a crude, unimaginative way. I didn't factor in S & M or KY Jelly just yet.

Drug stores carried quite a few "girly" magazines back then, but it took a quarter and some fairly good-sized cojones to sidle up to the counter and buy a copy. I had to talk about this to the priest on my next confessional trip, but it gave me an introduction to Bettie Page, a vixen to die for, as well as other nameless and shameless hussies.

You must realize that Hugh Hefner had not yet founded *Playboy* and we young 'uns found it difficult to imagine what a nude woman might look like. I truly wondered if I would ever see one. But as time passed more and more graphics of the opposite sex hit the market, and I gave thanks, along with thousands of other filthy little boys. Indeed, Hefner chose Bettie page for his second Playmate of the Month, Marilyn Monroe having been the first.

Miss Bettie Page her own self. She often appeared in a snappy little number called nothing. She made more money after she retired than she ever did dropping her laundry for dirty old men and almost as equally dirty little boys. From the author's dirty little collection.

A boy's early sex education might begin as mine did in outhouses, starting with exotic depictions of women in underwear in the Sears and Roebuck catalog. Sears published an annual mail order catalog about the size of a Manhattan phone directory, as did their rival, Montgomery Ward. Small boys often found most interest in the women's underwear ads, particularly those for brassieres and girdles. I came later to understand that brassieres helped stave off Cooper's Droop. (You can look it up.)

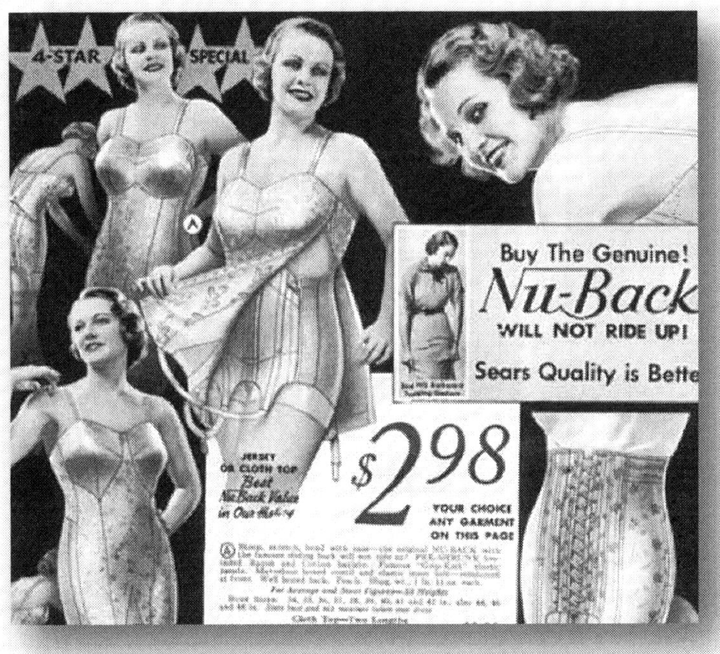

A girdle ad from a Sears and Roebuck 1938 catalog. The function of the flap the middle lady was opening escaped me, study and research it as I might. She looks pretty pleased about it, though. From the author's collection.

But I never did understand that girdle flap that the models opened so significantly, and I doubt many women wear such things nowadays. Such lingerie would lead to creeping mono-buttockism, not to be tolerated, but the basic concept of breasts emerged, and that started us down that long, slippery slope.

When our ductless glands began to ooze, we nasty little boys craved and needed all the information we could obtain, from any available source. There weren't a lot of sex manuals in the grade school library, and God knows The Teacher wasn't going to tell us anything. She did teach us "rape" as a word one day, but she didn't even hint at what it might mean, leaving us even more frustrated than before.

Life Magazine, surreptitiously examined while waiting for a physician or dentist, gave us wicked tykes other goodies to consider. In 1943 *Life* ran a photo of Chili Williams, a hottie with spectacular architecture who specialized in wearing polka dot bikinis.

Chili Williams as she appeared in Life Magazine. *The stuff of dreams. True, this bikini looks like a Mother Hubbard compared to the butt floss worn today, but in those innocent days we grooved on this image.*

The estimates vary, but *Life* received thousands of angry letters after publishing her picture. At age nine I didn't write any of them. Miss Williams passed on in 1993 at age eighty-two. May she rest in peace; she did a lot for me, decades before *Playboy* or *Penthouse* appeared on the grocery store racks.

Now, it's a matter of recorded fact (ah, yes, I remember it well) that for his first Playmate Hefner used a calendar nude of Marilyn Monroe. When that hit the stands, so did lots and lots of men and boys. But for the next Playmate The Grand Old Man of Tits went to a Merry Christmas shot of Bettie Page, the one and only, sitting on her heels in a Santa Claus hat and not another stitch, winking winningly at the camera. It must have been the first December issue. Later Bettie posed one morning with a wine hangover and two leopards. A former model turned photographer, Bunny Yeager, recorded the event. Should you care to celebrate Bettie's birthday, it's March 13.

I don't know how, but about this time a photography pamphlet showed up in our house, presenting the best shots of the previous year. One of them, by God, was a nude young lady, sitting back on her heels. I suddenly won the respect of my peers, and for only a few pence I would share this wonder with them. It added quite a bit to my reputation as a rustic *bon vivant.*

Not a lot of movie sex happened. The Hayes Code, which spelled out what was morally acceptable in a Hollywood film, went into effect in 1930 and was abandoned in 1967. A whole lot of people went to a lot of trouble to protect other people's morals. Who asked them?

When in 1943 a movie titled *The Outlaw* exploded across the land, all ecclesiastical hell broke loose. I have no idea where it got shown, certainly not in The Little Town Nearby. And they'd never let a nine-year-old in anyway, even if I could have gotten to the theatre. But sermons were preached against it and bibles issued to make sure no one saw it. It didn't work; entire crowds of people flocked to it.

I now possess a DVD of *The Outlaw* that some misguided soul gave me, but I cannot endure it. I don't consider the acting bad, necessarily, because I don't consider it acting at all. Jane Russell's glands would certainly make a Frenchman shout "*formidable*," or even "*pastèque*," and more epidermis showed than customary in those days. Looking back, I wish they had cast Kathryn Grayson as Rio. She wouldn't have needed to sing.

The Chemistry Set

As I said earlier, I intended to become a chemist in emulation of The Brother. He strongly encouraged this intention and went so far as to buy me a chemistry set, a folding box that contained small vials of various chemicals, an alcohol lamp, rudimentary scales, and a manual. I set up shop on the dining room table immediately, but The Mother soon put a stop to that when I burned holes in the tablecloth and generated hydrogen sulfide. Can we say, "rotten eggs"?

By the time The Brother actually went to work as a chemist and I prepared for high school, I had the basics of chemistry down pat. I could balance a formula with the best of them, albeit slowly. The Brother and I struck a deal. Since his lab contained all manner of chemicals not in my chemistry set, like sulfuric and nitric acid, I would donate blood for him in return for some chemical or other. He could use my blood as a normal, he thought. We found out I was chronically short of potassium in my blood, and I've been treated for that with a large pill daily ever since.

The Brother handled a needle very deftly indeed; he specialized in getting blood out of babies and kiddies without causing infantile hysteria. One day during an afternoon nap I awoke to find him drawing blood from my outstretched arm; he wanted to see if he could do that without waking me. I had no objection, but the experience startled me. Later in college I learned to take blood from my arms and then type it. Females in the class tended to squeal and faint, but the instructor seemed somewhat impressed with me. As I remember, two frat boys also squealed and fainted, but I didn't know them.

Opiate for the Masses

While The Father never attended church except for funerals or weddings, he took off as much of Sunday as he could. But The Mother, ever vigilant for signs of moral decay in her youngest child, always rousted me out for church. I didn't realize how dangerous the church could be till years later. I don't recall beginning to go to church with her; I suppose she starting hauling me as a helpless babe in arms. At any rate I began to look around to examine this new place. A doddering old priest, devoid of humor or Christian charity, presided over lengthy masses, often high masses, invariably in Latin, which I didn't speak very well at age six.

I used up my last crying jag when The Mother decided upon my sixth birthday that I should sit down in the front two rows with other children, where sermons could spill over us undiluted. I found no joy in that. I didn't know any of those kids, so I cut loose with the tears, no doubt embarrassing her terribly, but I sat up front for years to come. When I learned to recognize "*Ite, missa est*" as Latin for "Go, the mass is ended," I stood up to escape, trying to guess the Latin for "I'm outta here!"

One of the more imaginative nuns had a moment of miraculous revelation. She fantasized that I should join the church choir, the group who sang and tittered in the balcony while an organist wheezed out a lame accompaniment. I gave it a go; I didn't want to sing especially, but it would get me off the front row, anyway, and away from the oak kneeling rails which every pew had downstairs. After I had departed those hallowed halls, they renovated the entire place and even padded those accursed rails.

This photograph shows the interior of the church to which The Mother dragged me for about a decade and a half. Photograph by the author.

The Nun handed me a hymnal full of music that I couldn't read, with the lyrics in Latin, which I also couldn't read. I tried singing softly, but not softly enough. The nuns soon banished me from their choir. I felt a little like Adam being driven from The Garden of Eden by some dude with a flaming sword. Yeah, I felt that way, but not for very long.

I returned, happily, to the front row downstairs. No one would sit by me. I gave up sobbing as counter-productive. It registered frustration nicely, but to no end.

Then the establishment inflicted Sunday School on me. This new abomination involved going to the choir loft after the service; various nuns met us up there in order to change our ways. The sisters wore the old-style starched costumes, black and white habits. Very weird; I didn't know anyone else who dressed like that, even on Halloween.

Like the priest, the nuns had no discernible sense of humor. For kicks they drilled prayers into us: "Our Father," "Hail Mary," "Glory Be," (a sort of ecclesiastical trifecta) and later "The Apostle's Creed," "The Act of Contrition," and some others I forgot as soon as I could. When I got pretty slick with those, they hit me with the Ten Commandments, or at least one version of them. We learned the names of the sacraments and the seven deadly sins. We found out there were Holy Days of Obligation, which required our attendance at Mass, even if they didn't come on a Sunday. Next came the Catechism, a pamphlet given to us to memorize. The Catechism explained all about how to know, love, and serve God, and what you had to do to get to Heaven. Overall the odds seemed pretty slim for sinners like me, so I threw my copy into the creek about 1944. I tied a rock to it first, though, to make sure it didn't come back to haunt me.

The nuns told us all about some fictional little girl who lived an exemplary life but died young. This little darling had gone to Mass weekly and all that but had actually sinned once. She'd brought a shiny red apple to school one day, and some other little girl, less of a Christian, stole it and ate it, whereupon the perfect little girl slapped the snot out of her. I saw this as a completely reasonable response, not in the least sinful

But when the near-perfect little girl grew terminally ill, according to the nuns, she weakened and weakened and finally received the last rites, making a confession (she only had the one sin, but she got all the mileage out of it she could.) Then she did an Act of Contrition and packed it in and departed for Heaven and eternal bliss. Harps and wings and clouds and halos and all that jazz.

Well, that's what they told us. The story didn't seem likely to me, but I didn't argue about it. I failed to grasp any obvious point in all this, except maybe we should keep an eye on our apples. And the nuns seemed to savor describing hell to us, but they didn't do so well when they talked about Heaven; it came off a little vague and mushy. I wondered, for example, if people hunted squirrels or crows in Heaven, but I suspected they didn't. Not being totally simple-minded, I didn't ever ask the priest or the nuns about such matters.

Then they introduced us sinners to confession before we made our First Communion, about age seven, which the Church considered the age of reason. I was never sure of that, but again they made the rules, and as far as I knew they had the monopoly. I supposed the other guys I knew, Baptists and such, did pretty much the same stuff. Later I went to some Protestant ceremony and was stunned by the lack of fanciness.

I also had to be confirmed before I could go to confession and receive communion. Hell's clanging bells, I've been wanting some sort of confirmation for over seventy years now, but I guess they thought they'd gotten the job done back then.

Entering the confessional the first time fried my mind, I assure you. The confessional itself consisted of three cubicles, arranged in a row at the rear of the church. The priest sat enthroned in the middle cubicle, while we reprobates, oozing shame from every pore, lined up behind the back pew and slunk into one of the side cubicles when our turn came. Penitents knelt upon ubiquitous oak rails, facing a wooden screen. A panel slid open, allowing sinner and priest to chat about your particular depravities. What a treat. Clouding the issue, I knew the priest, since we only had one, and I figured he knew me and might call me out from the altar later in the morning. I was never eager to suffer public humiliation, so I hoped I would get lost in the crowd. On the other hand, I'm not all that sure the priest listened that carefully.

The confessionals in our church. The priest sat in the middle cell to hear an avalanche of small-town depravity. Sinners occupied the left and right cells. I always chose the right one, but I can't remember why. Photo by the author.

The sinner began with “Bless me, Father, for I have sinned,” then listed all the nastiness he or she had been up to since their last confession. If the priest listened, and I’m sure he had heard it all, short of worshipping graven images or satanic rites, he would then forgive you as a stand-in for God. The sinner wound up with an “Act of Contrition,” whereupon the priest inflicted some penance, usually the recitation of the Our Father and Hail Mary three times after returning to your pew. Then we exited in a purged and holy haze. In a state of grace, they told us. I never felt any different, but I kept still about that, too.

Now, I had problems with all this, sure enough. In the old days The Mother took me to confession on Friday afternoon, but if I planned to go to Communion Sunday that pretty well shot Saturday for any fun. I had to stay sin-free till I received Communion. You just tried to stay cool for about thirty-six hours, and the cycle could begin again. But it didn’t have to be that way.

But then I discovered that the priest held confessions just before the early (8:00 a.m.) Sunday Mass, so you could go spill your beans about 7:30. Then Communion would happen about an hour later, so not sinning became relatively simple, unless The Sex Goddess attended that particular Mass. When I learned about occasions of sin, which they insisted I should avoid, it dawned on me that The Sex Goddess probably qualified. I aspired to joining her on one of those occasions, but she seemed to be out of my range, just like those triple-damned crows.

Other problems arose. The confessionals lacked adequate soundproofing, so as I waited for the priest to get around to me, I often heard lurid details related by the person on the other side. This certainly entertained me, sometimes educated, and on occasion inspired. I once considered that if I could hear them, probably they could hear me, so I might invent something that would really frost their pumpkins, but that seemed indiscreet, no matter how tempting a prospect. After all, our immortal souls were at stake. Right.

After a few years it also dawned on me that some of the girls, less perfect than She of the Apple, stayed in the confessional longer than others. I further deduced that they must have more to confess. Hmm. And, hmm. I recall clocking a rustic bit of cuteness and finding her the champion sinner, time-wise. I didn't know quite what to do with this information.

Later I did. Fat lot of good it did me.

Since I wasn't of age, The Mother drove us to church. She didn't care to miss any Holy Days of Obligation, as they called them, so we made Good Friday services every year. I hated that one; three hours of kneeling on oak rails from noon to three o'clock, the same timetable as the actual Crucifixion, they told us. How exactly they knew this chronology didn't come up in any the conversations I heard about it.

But then one glorious year the priest announced that the service would not last three hours any more. The church officials cut it to about forty-five minutes, having decided the medieval guys did it that way. I wanted to whistle and cheer and stomp my feet, but my self-control got the better of me.

Sure enough, in less than an hour we headed for home. I gave thanks, silent ones.

But The Mother, never an advocate of change, complained that this innovation didn't seem necessary to her. I agreed, saying I wished to gee-minny they wouldn't keep changing the services every six or seven hundred years because I just couldn't keep track of them. That kind of lip wouldn't do, and I got slapped around while we went down the highway, which I found a small price to pay. I'd done it before, I assure you. One has one's priorities. And to thine own self be true, and all that.

But Church usually only happened on Sundays, with some exceptions, and thus I lolled around on the farm till The Little Country Grade School entered my life and began to clog up my days.

The BSA

The Church caused one dandy thing to happen to me; it sponsored a Boy Scout troop that met one evening a week, and The Parents approved thereof. Well, The Father didn't object to it, and The Mother thought the proximity to The Church would do me a world of good. So they made arrangements for me to be toted into the meetings weekly. I dug it.

The best part of the whole thing was that the meetings took place in town, in a house next to The Church. A civilian Scout Master led us, and the troop devoted time to learning knots and outdoor cooking and thinking pure thoughts and such.

A high point of my scouting career came when The Church sponsored a two-week summer camp, clear to hell and gone into the Ozark Mountains. The Parental Units anted up the necessary funds.

A few parents drove us to the Ozark campgrounds, where we stashed our gear and selected our bunks. I considered all this a total gas, novelties I'd never before imagined. Yes, we had hills at home, but the Ozarks had mountains. True, not very big ones.

The troop ate in a mess hall, savoring our heaps of mashed potatoes liberally laced with potassium nitrate. That chemical, the leaders thought, dampened any lustful desires we might have. Apparently not, they discovered one of my friends jerking his gherkin in the shower room and sent him home in shame. I doubt it cured him. Let's face it, as The Rancher would have said (you'll meet him later), we were all as horny as two-peckered billy goats.

We spent days at crafts; I made a bow, for example, and shot arrows with it, almost never hitting anything. We tested for merit badges; enough of them and a Scout moved up a rank or so. We got the badges for demonstrating our ability to swim, do photos, write essays, tie knots, hike, and so on.

Hiking took up a bit of time; the Scout Master would lead us down some trail. I recall a hell of a high cliff we inspected, perhaps one hundred feet top to bottom. Locals called it "Deer Leap," so I imagine some Bambi or other did a Peter Pan off it. Several of us did something else off it until the Scoutmaster made us quit.

The Scout Master also taught us how to play five-card stud poker, even though the Scouts didn't offer a merit badge for that. He admitted I showed a certain talent for the game. As the years went by I had to agree. I even began to realize when someone was a better player than I was, which saved me tolerable amounts of money.

My scouting career led to one other incident of considerable diversion. Having a small Brownie camera I decided to try for a merit badge in photography. I snapped away at small animals on our farm, but then one day while we were baling hay we scared up a four-foot bull snake. A harmless creature, but I thought it perfectly photogenic. I captured it by grabbing it behind its head, whereupon it wrapped itself around my arm as snakes are wont to do.

I explained to The Father that I needed to photograph it, and he agreed I could go get my camera.

So I hot-footed it to the house to get my Brownie from my bedroom. When I got there The Mother was napping, so I eased into my bedroom with the bull snake still wrapped around my arm. As I dug out the camera a squall like that of a scalded banshee went off behind me; The Mother had come in to see if I wasn't up to something she should make me quit.

When my pulse returned to normal (I didn't know about the snake's) I went out to the yard, unwound the reptile, and took my photos. The snake raced off to find someplace where this sort of outrage didn't happen and escaped before The Mother found her hatchet.

As I recall I got the merit badge. Just like the pickle back in Chapter One.

So, some diversions we made for ourselves, but Hollywood and the radio industry supplied a lot of it. If you'd like to know more about that, just dig into the next chapter.

CHAPER THREE

MIDWESTERN MEDIA, OR, THE LONE RANGER RIDES AGAIN!

We received mail once a day, about noon, delivered by a postman with a minor political appointment. We could count on *The Local Daily Newspaper* arriving in this mail; the man brought the edition from the previous evening about noon. I didn't ordinarily get any mail, but some interesting things might arrive. *Capper's Weekly* and *The Farm Journal,* both still publishing, which were sort of how-to magazines about farming, featuring such articles as "Hurray for Soy Beans!" or "Lespedeza Everywhere!" All of this came to our mailbox a quarter of a mile up our lane, but I devoured every copy as soon as I learned to read, meanwhile fantasizing about more exotic literature.

Battery-Powered Radio

Our major connection to the outside world, though, remained the radio. We huddled around the set more closely after The Brother shipped out, and we grew steadily more sophisticated about information from the South Pacific. I read recently that God created war to teach Americans geography. If He did, it worked.

Of course, we continued to listen to our favorite country/western performers: Dude Hank, The Hoosier Hot Shots, and The Duke of Paducah. The Duke always ended his gig by yelling "I gotta get back to the wagon, boys; these shoes are killin' me!" Class acts, all of them.

I also learned later that David Sarnoff, the head of RCA and NBC, determined radio network policy guaranteeing that Americans would get news programs whether they wanted them or not. I don't recall whether I actually heard news reporter Edward R. Murrow during the London Blitz or if I've just heard it played back so many times I think I did, but England stood alone against the Nazis in those days after France went under.

The radio supplied our chief form of amusement, as well, although sneaking up on outhouses and listening to people break wind remained an unbeatable source of hilarity. But the radio gave us on Monday, Wednesday, and Friday evenings at 6:30 "The Lone Ranger," with his great horse Silver and his faithful Indian companion, Tonto. The program's theme, the "William Tell Overture," could raise the dead, and later I discovered they also used Liszt Preludes, but whatever, I knew full well that no one had ever created better music. I admit to a brief flirtation with Khachaturian's "Sabre Dance," but mostly I remained true to William Tell. Even the Spike Jones version (let's just say Spike was a musical satirist) couldn't weaken my admiration.

The Father liked to listen to "The Lone Ranger," too, which further peeved The Mother. She seemed to think if anyone liked a thing and she didn't, it must weaken the other person's moral fiber and need immediate outlawing. The first time I ever heard her swear happened when the announcer proclaimed that night's episode of "The Lone Ranger" would be the one thousandth broadcast. The Father and I savored this historical thunderbolt, but The Mother grumbled "Yes, and I've heard every God-damned one of them!" Neither The Father nor I saw fit to comment or look at one another.

A publicity photo of The Lone Ranger and Tonto. I could only imagine their appearances listening to the radio, but these guys looked OK. So did their horses. From the author's collection.

She would have become ecstatic had someone told her "Tonto" was Spanish for "idiot."

But The Mother scheduled her own days around her favorite radio soap operas: "Young Widder Brown" (not "Widow," but "Widder"), "Ma Perkins" (an especially saccharine narrative that never reached resolution), and others of that ilk. I noted after a bit that the stories never went anywhere; they just kept on, the same as TV soaps today. Having mulled this over, I proposed to The Mother that she didn't need to listen every day; she could just tune in once a week or maybe once a month and easily catch up. I don't think she bopped me, but neither did she cotton to my suggestion.

An advertisement for some hustle for Jack Armstrong, the All-American Boy. Cute little booger, isn't he? Lots of boys wanted to be him. From the author's collection.

Other programs, far beyond our experience, came into our home. "Inner Sanctum" presented horror stories that curdled one's blood; we never listened to it. I reveled in the kiddy equivalent of soaps, fifteen-minute programs after school and after the soaps: "Jack Armstrong, The All-American Boy," my loyalty to whom won me the plane ride. "Hop Harrigan, The Ace of the Airways" flew around during World War Two. Hop had for a sidekick a doofus named Tank Tinker, strong, but dumb, really dumb. Dumb to perfection. Hop and Tank once crashed and were floating around in some ocean, and I began to sweat out how they could be saved. Alas, President Franklin Delano Roosevelt died April 12, 1945, and the radio stations took Hop and Tank off the air for three or four days. I thought it probably a plot by grownups to keep kids subjugated to higher authority.

Captain Midnight, leader of the Secret Squadron, who flew around World War II doing good deeds for everyone except the Germans and Japanese. From the author's collection.

Every Monday through Friday afternoon I also enjoyed the radio version of "Superman," an old favorite from the comic books. Tom Mix, an actual person, had a fifteen-minute show as well. "Captain Midnight" also migrated over from comic books. I once met an old actor who had played Captain Midnight on the radio, but by then no one cared, not even me.

But for my money the radio comedians led all competitors; their recordings still play well for modern audiences. Sunday nights offered the great ones; Jack Benny at six o'clock; I especially enjoyed the drunken bandleader, Phil Harris, and thought I might like to be like him when I grew up. Fred Allen followed Benny; if you look up "acerbic" in a 1940 dictionary you won't find a picture of Fred Allen, but you should have. A wonderful commentator on the human comedy. Or melodrama. Or farce.

The cast of the Jack Benny radio show, a favorite. Benny is third from the right. The woman is Benny's wife, Mary Livingstone. The man on the far right is Mel Blanc, a genius of galactic dimensions. Third from the left is Phil Harris, a booze-soaked bandleader.

ASIDE: I always enjoyed comedy, just for laughs, but came later to realize it wasn't just entertaining; human freedom demanded it. Indeed, in Harvy Mindess' insightful LAUGHTER AND LIBERATION, long out of print, I found a kindred soul. I gave thanks.

I should also mention a Saturday morning half-hour program called "Let's Pretend." A woman named Nila Mack produced it for Cream of Wheat, hot breakfast gruel with the consistency and taste of wallpaper paste. Even so, the stories, mostly adaptations of fairy tales, could be fun, especially those with ogres and monsters and trolls and other social misfits.

"Let's Pretend" started with everyone singing the theme song, "Cream of Wheat is so good to eat." The show lacked the masculinity of "Superman" or "Captain Midnight," though I'm not sure Nila Mack did. It offered the only radio action for kiddies on a Saturday morning.

For what it's worth, Nila Mack is buried in a town about ten miles south of The Little Town Nearby. I went to see her grave once. No big deal.

But her scrapbook in the Lincoln Center Theatre Collection in New York City is falling apart as she fades into oblivion.

My favorites included Edgar Bergen and Charlie McCarthy, the only time I ever heard of a ventriloquist starring on radio . . . think about it. Bergen, a mild-mannered sort of fellow, shared the stage with Charlie, a raucous, horny, irreverent, little dude complete with top hat, tuxedo, and monocle. His enemy threatened him with all manner of destruction, said enemy being W.C. Fields, who like many other comics of the day, and even now, got their laughs from strong drink and their incapacity for dealing with it. Fields got good responses by threatening to throw a termite on Charlie. His love of strong spirits garnered him lots of laughs, but not from The Mother.

Edgar Bergen protecting Charlie McCarthy from W.C. Fields and his saw. From the author's collection.

Another primetime program during the week was "Grand Central Station," which opened with a train chugging into Grand Central Station in New York City. Every week some rube came to New York from the outlying districts, and his or her adventures began immediately. I wondered as a kid what Grand Central Station actually looked like; I conjured up an edifice combining the best of the Parthenon, Taj Mahal, Oz, and Mayan temples. I suffered sore disappointment when I eventually found myself in the real building, but I had to admit it sure would have held a lot of hay. The few times I rode into or out from Grand Central Station I learned how efficient the designer had made it.

ASIDE: The radio thus gave us a bit of information from beyond. Not much, often distorted, but definitely better than nothing. As it happens, I recently received from my sister-in-law a web site with dozens of radio programs on it, recordings from the old days. The URL is "WWW: BEFORE TELEVISION . . . THERE WAS RADIO." Enjoy.

One rainy Saturday afternoon I learned that the radio gods planned to broadcast an honest-to-God opera in honest-to-God English. I decided to upgrade my cultural level and settled down for *Peter Grimes*. Well, the singers sang it in English; they might as well have sung it in Medieval Urdu for all I understood. I found out later that opera originated because of Renaissance misconceptions of the ancient Greek and Roman dramatic metric structures; those guys thought the plays should be sung. I rejected the whole silly business, although I've since suffered through a few operas.

I remember reading in a copy of *Popular Science* that someday we would be able to enjoy a thing called television, which would send pictures and audio through the air. I had my doubts. Eventually I actually bought a set for The Parents, a seventeen-inch model. They thanked me, and then traded it in the next day for a twenty-five-inch model. As I recall we got about two and a half channels, depending on which way the wind blew. Literally. And that was after The Brother had risked life and limb and I don't know what else crawling on top of the house to install a television antenna. You hardly ever see an antenna any more, but in those days getting reception required such devices.

Movies

Hollywood could have filled Fort Knox with the cash they made feeding our fantasies, mostly about World War Two. I don't know how many times I stiffened slightly, slumped over, and then collapsed, picked off by a Jap sniper, but I did it often and performed it fairly well. The Teacher didn't care for such competition, though.

The local opera house once upon a time hosted traveling shows but offered only movies by my time. When The Sister moved away, The Parents started taking me to movies. When I started going to it in high school I discovered there was this balcony. . . . Courtesy of the Cowley County Kansas Historical Museum.

Nowadays when you go to a movie you sit through a half hour of deafening previews. In our days we got some previews, certainly, but we also had newsreels, black and white footage of world events.

We also always got a cartoon. A Woody Woodpecker cartoon sent kids trooping out to the lobby for sugar goodies since we didn't dig him, but if Bugs Bunny or Tom and Jerry appeared we kept our seats and roared our approval. Bugs rejected all authority. Years later I met some guys from the Bronx who reminded me of Bugs, only they weren't quite as smart. Tom and Jerry's ongoing battles delighted me, as did the Roadrunner and Wile E. Coyote a bit later. Of all such cartoons, though, "What's Opera, Doc?" still leads the pack, followed closely by "The Barber of Seville" and "One Froggy Evening" featuring "The Michigan Rag." That rag sounds like a golden oldie, but it appears nowhere but in "One Froggy Evening."

You could look it up.

Once I literally fell out of my aisle seat during a Tom and Jerry cartoon; Tom had somehow changed a wing-table into a flying machine of sorts, using it to bomb Jerry with watermelons. Even at that early age I recognized and appreciated perfection of dramatic form.

I loved those cartoons, though, and I wouldn't dream of outgrowing them. Mel Blanc, a towering genius, deserved to go to Actors' Heaven with Laurence Olivier, both masters of their craft. Blank died 10 July 1989; Olivier the next day. They should have marched in together, Olivier doing Hamlet and Blanc doing Elmer Fudd. Or they might, for that occasion, have switched roles. When I die and go to heaven, I want to see Olivier do Elmer Fudd.

Back then filmmakers squeezed more money out of kids by cranking out serials. Made on a budget of possibly several hundred dollars, these episodic little dandies, studies in black and white, perhaps fifteen minutes long, ran twenty or thirty episodes. Superman once again led the pack for me, but various other beefy actors doing Captain America or Captain Midnight almost always got into impossible situations. Villains would tie up the hero and stack dynamite around him, light the fuse, and then skedaddle and watched the explosion from afar, at which point the episode would end. Next week we would be back in our places to learn that, by golly, our hero had escaped his bonds and eased on out the back door just before the explosion. We marveled and wondered if our hero's cleverness had any limits whatsoever.

We kids acted out these serials during school recesses. I began to discover it was more fun playing villains than heroes.

I was only four years old when The Sister started taking me to movies. *The Wizard of Oz*, for example, in 1939, in which The Wicked Witch of the West gave me nightly fantods. And *Bambi,* which led to blubbering and sobbing. Not by me, by The Sister.

She also took me to *Fantasia*. That Mickey Mouse movie featuring "Night on Bald Mountain" in 1940 probably stunted my growth. I eventually grew to six feet three, but if The Sister hadn't exposed me to that movie I might have starred in the NBA.

Later I think The Father ruled on what movies we'd see; they tended toward Westerns and Jeanette MacDonald-Nelson Eddy opuses. I now suspect that those MacDonald-Eddy musical sugar lumps made me the diabetic I am today.

Seeing *Jesse James*, starring Tyrone Power and Henry Fonda, fed my fantasy life for years. That film contained much shooting and killing, a veritable mother lode for future grade school recesses. The Mother totally hated it; it depicted Ozarkers, whom she held in utter contempt since she wasn't one.

But she endured the movie as best she could. As we headed for the lobby, we heard theme music behind us. The Father turned to look back, and then and there we all found out *The Return of Frank James* had just started, and The Father and I wouldn't have missed it for pie. The Mother spat fire in all directions, but she stayed the course. She had to or walk home.

They took me along to another oater, *My Darling Clementine*, again with Fonda, but enhanced by the muscular talents of Victor Mature as the tubercular Doc Holliday. I grooved on it. We came to the scene in the pouring rain when Fonda as Wyatt Earp swears vengeance over the body of his kid brother in Arizona, and The Father whispered to me, "It wouldn't rain that way in that country." I remain impressed by him to this day, even if I have since seen it rain very heavily indeed down there.

My Darling Clementine was OK as a western movie, if you didn't know what really happened. For example, Doc Holliday didn't die during the Gunfight at the OK Corral; he died in bed years later. For that matter that gunfight wasn't at the OK Corral; it was on Fremont Street. And Wyatt Earp and his brothers didn't get to Tombstone by driving a herd of cattle to California. I became a purist about such things as the truth-seeker I was. Hollywood will really mess you up if you're not careful.

But for all-time impact *The Uninvited* remains the stud horse of my early cinematic experience. Starring Ray Milland, filmed in England, this film contains an honest-to-God ghost, an ectoplasmic creature flopping around in a literally haunted house. As a kid I didn't see the actual movie, but I accidentally saw the previews, which scared the absolute obscenity and vulgarity out of me. For the next several weeks I slept under the covers with only one eyeball and one nostril partially exposed to a world saturated with evil. I imagined my immediate vicinity rife with king freaks in 3-D, all of them eager to rip and tear and savor my tender young flesh. If I accidentally fell asleep, the dreams that came to visit were truly surreal.

I have met grown-up people who firmly believe in ghosts and angels and aliens and God only knows what else. I kind of hope there are aliens; we might learn something.

Comic Strips

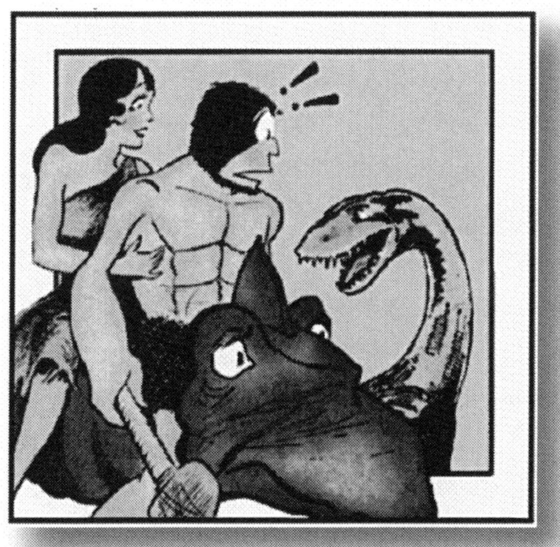

Alley Oop with his main squeeze, Ooola, riding on their pet dinosaur, Dinny. Did it matter that humans and dinosaurs never coexisted? Don't be silly. I mean, who knew? From the author's collection.

The Father used to read to me the comic strips from *The Local Daily Newspaper*. I loved "Alley Oop" by V. T. Hamlin, the unlikely saga of a caveman with a pet dinosaur. I didn't realize that humans and dinosaurs never lived at the same time, and I wouldn't have cared if I had. Oop's girlfriend, a busty hussy named Ooola, writhed around in a ragged hide sarong. In fact, Ooola looked a lot like Bettie Page, but she predated her by geological ages.

"Dickie Dare," another strip, featured a kid who ripped around getting into various escapades. In one episode a native witch doctor with an awful looking mask appeared at a window to scare the liver out of Dickey Dare. I don't recall what it did for young Dickie, but it sure did the job on me; that shaman perked up my dreams for months afterward. I would try to force myself not to think about it. I never had much luck with that, though, but eventually the horror faded.

The Witch Doctor from the comic strip, "Dickie Dare." This dude gave me horrific dreams for a few weeks, I assure you. From the author's collection.

In time I discovered that Milton Caniff who had created "Dickie Dare" later became a tremendously successful cartoonist, producing "Terry and the Pirates" and "Steve Canyon." He also did a definitive cartoon after the JFK assassination, which depicted Abraham Lincoln slumped over, head in his hands, in the Lincoln Memorial.

Caniff also created popular characters during World War Two: Willie and Joe, two grimy dog-faces slugging it out in the European Theatre of Operations. You can find them in a book titled *Up Front,* and I recommend it most heartily. Out of print, but you can scare up a copy, I'm sure.

My all-time favorite comic strip, though, remains "Li'l Abner," by Al Capp.

Abner reached hitherto inconceivable levels of heft and stupidity. His lady friend had a different appeal; Daisy Mae cavorted around and about in a shredded micro-mini. Capp's villains, the Scraggs, also delighted me no end. True, they resembled some of our neighbors, perhaps a mere coincidence. Perhaps not. Capp achieved an overall effect of anarchy and disrespect for all authority, thus endearing himself to small boys, outlaws, and nut cases everywhere.

Al Capp provided a cast of characters that surpassed everything I'd ever seen or heard tell of: Joe Btfsplk, who suffered under a literal cloud of bad luck for his entire life; Stupefyin' Jones, a lady whose raunchiness truly stupefied, even more than Abner's blonde whoopsie; Senator Phogbound, who matured into Senator Claghorn on the Fred Allen show, as well as Foghorn Leghorn in the movie cartoons. Capp also gave us the ever-popular Earthquake McGoon, a hulking, villainous lout. These characters haven't vanished, although Capp did; all those characters and more flourish on the Internet, to my utter delight.

Li'l Abner, every bit as dumb and happy as he looked. Behind him are Mammy and Pappy, his miniscule parents, and his busty blonde babe, Daisy Mae. From the author's collection.

Alas, Capp grew political and replaced his comic genius with dry social commentary. The strip lingered for a time, then slid out of sight, although a Broadway musical, based on the strip, ran a moderately successful 693 performances. I still hear of Sadie Hawkins Day Celebrations taking place here and there; I even participated in some of them. Sadie Hawkins Day became a spring festival during which women and girls pursued men and boys; Daisy Mae took dead aim on Li'l Abner. At high school dances girls would ask boys for dances, and if they weren't careful, they might get them. I don't know if offspring ever resulted, but I wouldn't be surprised. I believe the practice has fallen out of favor.

The comic strip first appeared in 1934 and finished up in 1977. That's a long run, folks.

Comic Books

Kids in those days loved comic books; we bought, read, traded, stole, and collected them, and those ten-cent booklets inspired many of our kiddy games, to the dismay of our parents. We kids watched in horror as The Mother and others like her discarded them as trash. They were just that, of course, but trash can be treasure, too.

Scholars have amassed entire histories of the comic strips and comic books. For a dime, one slim dime, the tenth part of a dollar, I could enter into a world of fantasy, eroticism, and World War Two and thrill to the exploits of the various superheroes, mortal or immortal. I dug it the most. So did my colleagues.

Conjuring up a short list of my favorites evokes wonderful memories even today. Superman, certainly, led all the superheroes. Something about the Man of Steel appealed to us; he outsold all the others. And he still does. "Action Comics, No. 1," which introduced Superman, cost ten cents when it appeared in the 1930s, but a mint copy recently sold at auction for over three million dollars.

Batman lurked in the darkness, and as a mere human he could get hurt, and did, adding another layer of apprehension for both him and me. Billy Batson, a boy, became Captain Marvel when he uttered the magic word: "Shazam!" This word endowed Captain Marvel with the wisdom of **S**olomon; the strength of **H**ercules; the stamina of **A**tlas; the power of **Z**eus; the courage of **A**chilles; and the speed of **M**ercury, mushing together Greek mythology and the Bible, to the detriment of both.

Captain Marvel with his other self, Billy Batson. Billy would transform into the Captain whenever he said "Shazam," then he'd kick the coon dog doo-doo out whoever needed it. Small boys dreamed of such powers. From the author's collection.

He had for an enemy a little green worm, Mr. Mind, possessed of a towering intellect. Amazing. All the worms I ever grew acquainted with seemed pretty stupid, as in brainless.

But now let us speak of Plastic Man, a hero transformed into a humanoid who could shape shift, that is, transform himself into any shape he wanted. Think about it. Some fellow aficionados considered this a little far-fetched, but I bought the bit.

Plastic Man, a shape-shifter from way back. The cumquat in the polka-dot shirt is his faithful sidekick, Woozy Winks. From the author's collection.

How, I hear you ask, did he achieve this astonishing plasticity? Well, he fell into a vat of chemicals in some factory or other, the same as The Joker did in the Batman stories. But whereas The Joker, who was a gangster to begin with, only gained a grotesque grinning visage, which was within the bounds of a strained reality, Plastic Man got the whole nine yards, total elasticity. Where he got his pretty red suit I don't recall, but it flexed with him.

But for some reason he had a total sap running around with him, a Mr. Woozy Winks. I don't remember how he came to be Plastic Man's buddy, and I think Old Stretch might have done far better, but this seemed to be a pattern for superheroes of the day.

The special effects people couldn't quite achieve the illusion of Plastic Man's plasticity, so that particular hero never made it to the silver screen.

I don't think anyone missed him, especially. I certainly didn't.

As I entered a preternaturally erect adolescence, I began to have some suspicions. Eventually I read about the Spartans in ancient Greece and their propensity to fight in what we might call pairs; a young man and an older one.

Recalling my childhood heroes, I note that a lot of those super guys ran around with adolescent boys. Superman seemed straight, certainly; Lois Lane took precedence over Jimmy Olson. Captain Marvel remained a boy until he said the magic word. But Captain America had Bucky, a smaller version of himself. Batman had Robin to back him up. Even Plastic Man palled around with his goofus, Winky.

I understand that a hero needs a sidekick, what the French call a *confidante.* Someone to talk to, to discuss the plans for the day and so on. Hamlet needs Horatio, doesn't he? Well, doesn't he? Some say Hamlet does a nice job of talking to himself several times during that play. Does the line "To be or not to be?" have a familiar ring? There are others.

And then it dawned on me that cowboys did the same thing. The Lone Ranger traveled with Tonto, the Indian who had nursed him back to health after some baddies left him for dead. Other cowboys apparently went to Central Casting and auditioned mental defectives for traveling companions. Roy

Rogers had Gabby Hayes to fill in while Dale Evans fed the horses, for example. Gene Autry, loathed by my generation, picked up Pat Butram somewhere along the trail. "Have another stick of Doublemint, Gene," and like that. Melody Ranch. Phooey. Double Phooey.

ASIDE: Throw another log on the fire whilst I relate a yarn. During high school another guy and I went to our local theatre to see something or other one evening, the second half of a double feature. The first feature, alas, starred Gene Autry. We slumped down and endured as best we could until the heroine gave Old Gene a tongue-lashing and started to ride off. Gene whipped it out—his guitar—and began a ballad. Sure enough, the heroine's horse began to slow down, then stopped, and the girl looked back at Old Gene, then came a-moseying back to him. My friend and I, budding drama critics, couldn't take it; we hooted and hollered and proposed loudly that it was the horse, not the girl, who had a doughnut for Big Gene. The management ejected us into a warm summer evening to find other forms of recreation, which we did. We were needed, but not appreciated.

My innate sense of charity and morality leads me to think the creators of this young-old concept wanted small boys to imagine they could go out and have adventures with heroes. I'm not at all sure we bought it, but that's what I imagine they promoted. But I don't think that's what the Spartans had in mind at Thermopylae in 480 B.C.

A heroic type of cowboy, Red Ryder, reached some sort of stardom, besides having BB guns named after him. I kid you not; he outdid every other buckaroo and obtained an Indian boy to join him in riding the range; a lad whose tribe had named him Little Beaver. Red befriended a local lady, Beth, a "gal pal," as he called her, but when it came time to chase the guys in the black hats, he chose Little Beaver for a sidekick.

Red Ryder (white hat), caught from behind by A Bad Guy (black hat), from whom he will be rescued by Little Beaver (no hat, but a feather). From the author's collection.

When The Mother got fed up and outlawed comic books from my life, I moped and pouted for a few days, then transferred my allegiance to Big Little Books, chunky publications with more text, but the same stories and some of the same heroes. The Big Little Books had more words in them than comic books; I suppose someone somewhere might have thought that would be good for us.

Hell's fire, we were reading, weren't we? For some of us it started a habit that never ended; if we started with Red Ryder we might end up with *Oedipus Rex* or *The Iliad.* I for one developed a passion for the printed word that never has left me, even though I had to occasionally read the backs of cereal boxes and copies of *Home Beautiful* while waiting for a doctor or dentist. I rest my case.

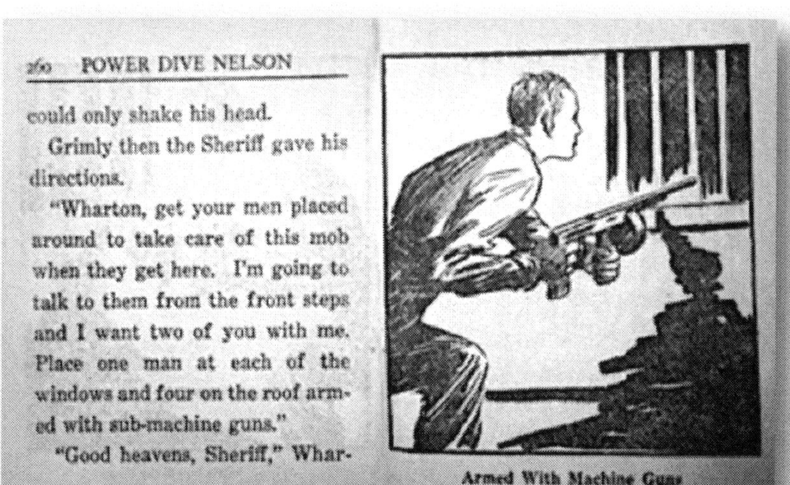

260 POWER DIVE NELSON

could only shake his head.

Grimly then the Sheriff gave his directions.

"Wharton, get your men placed around to take care of this mob when they get here. I'm going to talk to them from the front steps and I want two of you with me. Place one man at each of the windows and four on the roof armed with sub-machine guns."

"Good heavens, Sheriff," Whar-

Armed With Machine Guns

Two pages from a Big Little Book, as they called them. Typical dimensions for such books were 3 ¾" wide, 4 ½" tall, and 1 3/8" thick. Comic books were artistic masterpieces compare to Big Little Books; you could get an even money bet as to which was worse, the graphics or the text. But we were all rube kids, so what did we know? From the author's collection.

Eventually all the kids sneaked back to comic books; The Parents capitulated. Yes, we were smaller than they were, to be sure, but we outnumbered them, and we didn't have anything else to do but figure out ways to erode their authority. And the matter of comic books wasn't all that high on The Parents' priority lists, not like winning World War Two or getting everyone fed. So we waited it out, amusing ourselves with Big

Little Books, underwear advertisements, sexual fantasies, and smutty jokes we heard from the older guys.

Reading in General

After I learned to read I would immerse myself in any print I could locate. Newspapers got more interesting, and so did the books in the Grade School "library," and a few years later, the kiddy section of the Public Library in The Little Town Nearby. I loved reading and still do. Were my eyes to quit on me, I'd have to consider shuffling off this mortal coil. The Brother feels the same way about it, even at age ninety-seven.

He and The Sister also devoured print in almost any form. When I began to gobble up all the print I could find, The Mother exclaimed, "I wish I'd had one kid who couldn't read!" But she didn't, and we've all kept at it for the rest of our lives. All hail Gutenberg! All hail Aldus Manutius, who's never received the credit he should.

I urge you to look up Aldus about whom you should have learned in school. Start dropping his name into casual conversations, and perhaps we can start an Aldus Manutius Fan Club. Tee-shirts. Newsletters. Conventions.

The Telephone Party Line

The rural phone system supplied another source of amusement. Some government—city, county, township, whatever—ran telephone wires out into the country side, and somehow farmers secured phones, the old jobs that hung on the wall. A person had to walk up to it to use it.

Two large dry cells inside the wooden box supplied power. If you wanted to call a neighbor, you cranked the appropriate combination of long and short rings, which sent the signal winging through the wires to the aforementioned neighbor. Unfortunately, it sent the same signal to every other phone on your party line. We recognized our own incoming messages when we heard one long and three shorts; that signaled us to pick up and find out who wanted what and how much of it.

Lots of the country folk, starved for information and entertainment, listened in to other people's phone calls. Yes, they did, oh, my, how they did.

An old-style telephone, powered by dry cells. We made calls by cranking a handle on the right side of the unit, listening through the earpiece on the left, and speaking into the mouthpiece on the front. We thought we were some pumpkins when we later got one with a dial. Photo by the author.

By the time I was in high school and calling girls to chat them up I would hear the clicks as various farm wives picked up their phones to eavesdrop. Given the opportunity now, I might have given them information that could have triggered cardiac arrest if not miscarriage, but in those days I lacked sufficient information, experience, or even imagination. Readings from Henry Miller might have cured these audio-voyeurs. Over the years, though, I remembered we had books by Erskine Caldwell (*Tobacco Road*) or later, Mickey Spillane. Discussions of possible pregnancies or abortions might also have helped the old biddies fantasize. It would also have given them conversational material for their lifetimes, perhaps longer.

If you wanted to make a call of greater importance than to a mere neighbor, a long-distance call, for example, you rang one long ring to rouse the operator, then negotiated with her for what you wanted. That usually involved waiting while she placed the call and called you back. Such calls resembled telegrams, used only for the biggest of deals: babies, weddings, and deaths. What British genealogists call hatches, matches, and dispatches.

Not a great system, but it worked. It improved after World War Two, like lots of things. That war upped the economy and shook the United States out of the Depression doldrums, no question about it. It was a hell of a price to pay for economic recovery at the cost of millions of lives across the world. I wish we could have done it some other way.

Interaction with Neighbors

Not much socializing took place among farm families, but they would occasionally have a get-together. While the elders chatted on the porch, the kids would sneak upstairs and look in bureau drawers to see what they could find. Underwear always gave us a giggle, but I don't recall finding anything more entertaining.

I recall my uncle, The Swede, a fine man, hosting card parties for his neighbors. His house had a screened-in porch in which he and The Aunt would set up card tables for the games and prepare iced tea and such for refreshments. And a good time would be had by all.

With only one small problem. When we attended The Swede's pitch parties, as we always did, The Brother would lie on the fender and shoot jackrabbits while The Father drove. No problem there, but The Brother would then give the dead rabbits to The Swede's hound dogs, who would gobble them down in record time.

But then the hounds would sneak under the card tables and before long begin to ease out gasses of eye-watering toxicity. Green Creepers and Juicy Wet Ones would drive the card players from their tables, embarrassing The Swede no end. He'd drive the hounds off the porch like an archangel, but the hounds would come sneaking back after a couple of deals and continue their digestive processes.

The neighbors found all this hilarious. So did I, for that matter. Even The Mother had to smile a bit.

I recall visiting my best friend's house once and while waiting for him to finish some chores, complimented his clinically obese mother on how dirty her house seemed. She accepted the praise gracefully, I'll admit, but word got back to The Mother and once again she took me aside and spoke to me. Even as the epitome of cuteness, I sometimes lacked tact. I just wanted to be polite and make conversation like a good fellow.

One memorable year on the Little House on the Prairie, Part Two, The Mother and neighborhood ladies decided I should have a birthday party. So there came to our farm perhaps a dozen kids, scoured spotless, bearing wrapped presents, which they begrudgingly surrendered to me. I found it all quite a good deal, then proposed we all play “Superman” with me in the title role. I vanquished evil, and the other kiddies went back to their homes. I don’t recall another birthday party in that part of the county, though. Maybe they just didn't invite me.

A good many of our neighbors lacked even that much social grace. A pack of brothers lived to the south of us; when they came into The Little Town Nearby on a Saturday night, they usually looked for someone to fight. If they didn’t find anyone else, they’d fight each other. Their needs were simple.

So were they. One such evening one of them got tanked up on beer and decided to go swimming, so he dove off the railroad bridge over the river just south of town. By golly, he missed the river and went head first into a sand bar, breaking his neck. That didn’t kill him, though, and he was back the next Saturday sporting a neck brace, looking for a fight as usual. He found no takers. In time he healed up and returned to challenging one and all. I’ve tried to find out what eventually became of them, but no one seems to know. Or they’re just not telling.

But I was too young to partake in such festivities, and by the time I had gained enough years, those neighbors were gone, quite gone, not to be found.

Other Amusements

Our farm had a small creek running through it, and I often found business down there to keep me occupied and out of the work force. Several pecan trees dropped their bounty on gravel bars there, and two rocks will open a pecan as well as pliers or a hammer. For you city dudes, a pecan tree grows pecans, an edible nut about the size of the end of your thumb. You can also buy them in stores. They remain very popular among nut freaks; I even know a place in London in which you can order a slab of pecan pie, thus branding yourself as an American tourist.

Mulberry trees grew fruit infested with small insects, but still delicious, protein and all. Berry bushes taught me a small degree of patience; I ate the berries as soon as they became visible, not bothering with the concept of "ripe." Sensational stomach aches and paranormal diarrhea resulted, again rendering me unfit for servitude.

I got stupid when I found a hole in our house's foundation. Obtaining a flashlight, I crawled through said hole and discovered a layer of stone rubble beneath the house; we had no basement. I proceeded on.

We had plenty of snakes on our farm, including copperheads, all we needed, and some to spare. Why I didn't encounter one under the house I'll never know, nor what I'd have done when I did. Copperheads are both venomous and aggressive; I had one chase me during an encounter. I could outrun them, I'm happy to report. But then I was running on dry ground.

Had I found snakes or they had found me under the house I suppose I'd have done my best to rise up through the floorboards and seek diversions elsewhere. I don't think I could have done it, but I would have tried, damned straight.

Most of the snake population on our farm didn't pose any threat to anyone; they lacked the necessary venom to do anything fatal to any animals or humans.

And so the days came and went. The Sister married and reproduced; her first of four daughters delighted The Parents for a while, being their first grandchild. This child needed entertainment, as little childen do, and The Mother and The Sister ganged up on me and forced me to haul Creature One around in my little red wagon. I resented such intrusions into my time, but

I of course bore it with good will. Oh, shucky-durn, it might happen that I would take a corner too sharply and dump Creature One out on the hot, stony soil. This life is hard and cruel.

I of course confessed these sins, they being venial, not the more terrible mortal. The priest kept a straight face.

Barefoot Boy with Dynamite

My first experience with dynamite came after we had moved up to The Little House on the Prairie, Part Three. As previously described, inhabitants there used an outdoor privy for years. When we added running water we also added a bathroom, attached to the back of the house—tub, lavatory, stool, the whole shootin' match.

We needed a disposal system, though; no sewers ran from The Little Town Nearby five miles out into the country. We needed a septic tank, a large repository about eight feet in diameter and six feet deep with bacterial action to neutralize waste. Such a tank necessitated a large hole, and the ground on that hill consisted mostly of rocks; we figured the topsoil had all washed off shortly after the Mesozoic Era. Digging didn't sound like any fun at all. The Parents would have made me do it, but they didn't want to wait four or five years while I got the job done.

When The Brother returned from the Navy he got a job working for The Little Town Nearby as a lineman, and he plied that trade for a while. When it came time to make the hole in the hill he told us that the City used blasting mats, circular rugs six or eight feet across made of four-inch hawser. When excavating in town the crews placed the charge, then covered it with the mat before setting it off. This prevented them from blowing up nearby houses.

Since the site proposed for our septic tank lay about twenty feet from our house, The Brother borrowed one of those mats, then stopped by the hardware store and bought six sticks of dynamite.

In those days a citizen could walk into a hardware store and buy dynamite with no questions asked. Not kids, of course, but reasonable looking adults. I never tried to purchase any; the hardware clerks were too savvy.

When The Brother drove up to our house I greeted him as usual; he showed me the dynamite, which impressed me, but not so much as when he threw all six sticks up into the air. I supposed I would chat up Jesus that very day as I tried to catch them, and as I recall I caught a couple and was snapping my teeth at another when it hit the dirt.

I hadn't learned that dynamite needed detonators before it would explode, but it did. Called a blasting cap, the detonator contained fulminate of mercury, pretty unstable stuff. Some kids shoot these blasting caps out of their slingshots, often losing fingers and eyes but gaining valuable knowledge.

So The Father and The Brother picked the site for the tank and drilled a hole into the stony soil. Then they put blasting caps into a stick of dynamite and inserted it into the hole. The Brother covered the entire situation with the mat, lit the fuse, and we all retreated to a respectful distance.

When the charge went off it blew the mat about twenty feet straight up, and large stones flew into the air. When they came down, some of them on the roof of the house, The Mother appeared to suggest procedural refinements. We removed the loose rock and repeated the process with smaller charges, and eventually achieved a hole to be proud of. We inserted the tank and completed the plumbing, thereby joining the rural elite with our indoor john.

But God has a sense of humor, and we had some dynamite left over. All this happened in the middle of the summer with Fourth of July just ahead. My Swedish Uncle had a habit of celebrating the Fourth by finding a dead tree on his farm, fastening several sticks of dynamite to the highest limb, lighting a long fuse, and scrambling back down. *The Little Town Daily Newspaper* often ran stories on July fifth of a mysterious explosion southeast of town.

But The Uncle had passed away. In his honor, perhaps, The Father, The Brother, and the Brother-in-law decided to set off the remaining dynamite. I tagged along, of course. South of our house about a half-mile ran a dirt road a mile long with no houses on it. The men decided to put a half stick of explosive on top of a fence post, which they did, lit the fuse, and then we moved on down the road. As we stood there looking back at the post, I asked them what would happen if a car came by that post when the dynamite went off. My kinfolk just looked at me, albeit perhaps with a smidgen of newfound respect.

And did an auto indeed come toward us, passing the post with the charge on it? Yea, verily. They got fairly well past it before it went off. The car, which had California plates, identifying them as seriously lost, sped up a bit, then slowed down as it passed us. My relatives studied the pastures around us, bird watching, I suppose; the people in the car stared at us but chose not to do battle.

That day I learned that parents, big brothers, and grown people in general could pee in the chili, same as me. I found that information valuable; it has never left me. But it was a revelation in my young life, one every kid goes has, I suppose. On second thought, some of them never do figure it out, more's the pity.

Fishing with Dynamite

I wasn't quite done with dynamite, though. One summer a terrific drought hit our area, not an unusual event. Our Little Creek began to dry up; only a few of the deeper pools of water remained, and they threatened to disappear ere long.

I don't know who had the idea, but The Brother and I decided to dynamite the remaining pools between our place and The Uncle's, something like two miles of creek. This would kill the fish remaining in those pools, then we would distribute this bounty among our neighbors. Since the fish would die anyway, it seemed like (1) our Christian duty, and (2) fun, as in noisy.

We, or rather The Brother, devised a technique. We secured a number of pint fruit jars, doubtless from The Mother's stock, doubtless without bothering her about it, and punched holes in the lids. When we came to a likely pool, we'd put a cap and fuse into a quarter stick of dynamite, put the dynamite in the jar, pack gravel around it so it would sink, thread the fuse through a hole in the lid, and then screw the lid onto the jar. When ready we lit the fuse, tossed the bomb into the pool, watched it sink, and in a few seconds a rather satisfying explosion brought all the fish in the pool to the surface, belly up. We then collected them in baskets for later distribution.

And did this plan contain flaws? Yes, Lord, it did. Our scheme worked for a while, I must admit. Then we came to a pool with a steep bluff on one side, five feet high, with a little ledge at the bottom, a sort of miniature Omaha Beach. We prepared our lethal charge, but we couldn't find much gravel, so we substituted dirt. Dirt doesn't sink as well as gravel. As we squatted on the ledge, The Brother tossed our grenade into the pool and stared at it as it bobbed back up to the surface. We didn't take time to talk it over; we both launched ourselves up and over the ledge, cresting the top just as the charge went off, sending broken glass at high speed in all directions. Unharmed, we lay there, discussing the virtues of (1) more gravel and (2) longer fuses. We began to carry bags of gravel to make sure we didn't, as The Brother put it, have to start picking glass out of our ass.

Our family feasted on perch and bullheads for a week or more. We also supplied the neighbors with many fish. No loaves, but many fish.

The Raft

Not all our diversions in the country offered such high drama. I had eventually learned to read at The Country Grade School, but they didn't have many books there and none worth the effort, except the kiddy encyclopedia.

But one day The Parents went to another town, a clone of The Little Town Nearby; I have no idea why. While they shopped in a Woolworths, I meandered around and found a table full of books. I picked up one, and my life changed.

I had selected Mark Twain's *The Adventures of Huckleberry Finn.* You may have heard of it. This particular edition sold for a dollar. I don't know where I got it, but I had a dollar, so I made the deal and thus owned my first book, my very own.

I've bought thousands of books since then, but I've never found a better one. Sometimes you get lucky

I had, as has been my custom ever since, read a few paragraphs of the book before I bought it. God, I liked it; this was some funny stuff, and it happened on a river, not just a creek like we had. I had to buy it so I wouldn't hurt myself laughing in the store and have to be taken aside and spoken to.

I went through it rapidly the first time, and I loved the chapters when Huck and Jim drifted down the Mississippi and had their adventures. I immediately became a lifelong Twain fan, so I set out to emulate Huck. Huck had a raft; obviously I needed one, too. The Midwest lacked serious raft traffic in those days, but The Father had a stack of fence posts over by the barnyard; I asked him if I could have some to make a raft. He agreed. So I spent most of one summer constructing what I imagined as a raft. I lashed and nailed and wired together two layers of posts, then added several boards on top of that. Damned hard work, really, and The Father watched me bemusedly while I worked harder on that raft than I ever did on any of my chores.

I finished. The next part of the master plan involved putting my creation in The Little Creek. I had built my raft about two hundred yards from the nearest water of any significance. In hindsight I thought I could have taken the posts individually down to the water, but I didn't want to dismantle my raft. So I crowbarred and tugged and dragged and heaved and levered the raft, six feet square, down to a good-sized pool of water on The Little Creek.

The time came for launching and launch it I did. I suppose that thrice-accursed raft still lies at the bottom of that pool if floods haven't carried it downstream. I had constructed my vessel from green hedge posts, and green hedge floats about as well as The Statue of Liberty. I think The Father knew that as he watched me all summer, but he never said a mumbling word. Perhaps he thought I would never forget that lesson. Perhaps he was right.

But besides *Huckleberry Finn* other books drew my attention and fascinated me. *Treasure Island* happened pretty early, as well as the short story, "The Gold Bug." Then of course I discovered *The Adventures of Tom Sawyer,* and my cup ranneth over. I had discovered a gold mine of literary treasures that would see me through ensuing decades. I learned not to just read books, but to read authors. It was to rejoice.

Another Book of Significance

In those bygone days there existed in Detroit the headquarters of Johnson Smith & Company. I have before me a copy of a replica of the 1929 Johnson Smith & Co. Catalog, filled with ads for "Surprising Novelties, Puzzles, Tricks, Jokegoods, Useful Articles, Etc." This reprint appeared in 1970, published by Chelsea House Publishers in New York. On one page there is handwritten "From the Collection of Richard Merkin."

Well, it might have been, but a merkin is a pubic wig. You can look it up.

As a mere lad I had an earlier edition, but I have no idea how I came upon it. Perhaps I saw an ad for it in a comic book and sent away for it. Perhaps The Brother had a copy and passed it on to me, or I found it while rummaging around.

As the editor of the reprint proclaimed:

> *Johnson Smith is to Man's darker side what Sears Roebuck represents to the clean-limbed, soil-tilling righteous side. It is a rich compost heap of exploding cigars, celluloid teeth, anarchist "stink" bombs. The Johnson Smith Catalog is a magnificent, smudgy thumbprint of a totally lusty, vibrant, alive, crude post-frontier society.*

In other words, a boyhood dream come true. Yes, they sold rubber dog doo-doo and whoopee cushions, but just for openers. Where else could you get a .38 pistol, a real one, for six dollars? What public library could offer, as Johnson Smith did, a copy of "Brudder Gardner Stump Speeches: Comic Lectures and Negro Sermons"? For a quarter? Or to be fair, "Southwick's Irish Dialect Poems and Recitations" for thirty-five cents?

They sold stuff beyond imagination. Exploding donkeys for fifteen cents. Rubber hot dogs. Magic nose flutes. The Ventrillo, a device to throw your voice, only ten cents, sure to make you the life of the party.

But my favorite, the one I always wanted to order and never did, was the Wonderful X-Ray Tube, for a dime, three for a quarter, six bits a dozen. You could see through things with it, the ad claimed. I could think of several things I wanted to see through, but I hesitated to pay a dime for what I suspected might be a fraud.

But wonder of wonders! This company, while past its Golden Age, remains in business to this day, still in Detroit. They've surpassed themselves; they no longer offer the Wonder X-Ray Tube, but they have now, on the same page as the $0.99 Fart Bomb Prank Set, a set of the X RAY GLASSES! Best gag ever!

They described it as:

> *Amazing optical illusion glasses seem to give you X-ray vision. Apparently see bones through skin. Girls won't trust you, but let them look for themselves.*

Only $1.98. I haven't given up hope.

Other Books

As the years went by, I became more and more fascinated with books. In high school I discovered *The Complete Sherlock Holmes,* which totally engrossed me. I've accumulated several complete sets over the years.

And there came one wonderful day in The Small Town Nearby's only book store when I picked up a paperback copy of

I, the Jury and learned about Mike Hammer as created by Mickey Spillane. Well, I thought it an important book at the time. Maybe not now. I read all of the Mike Hammer books, just as in graduate school I read all the James Bond epics. Comics for grown-ups, let's face it.

A town lady visited our farm one day and saw me carrying a book; she inquired as to what I was reading. The Mother blushed to admit she had no idea what I read. But I was in like a porch-climber; I was toting a copy of *The Robe,* all about Jesus and the Romans, written by Lloyd C. Douglas. Hollywood made it into a Cinemascope hit and no doubt made Douglas many shekels indeed. Richard Burton dried out enough to play the lead, supported by the beefy Victor Mature.

The Catcher in the Rye came out, and I saw guys reading it who couldn't read a stop sign. A deserved hit. Some guys got to where they could quote Holden Caufield, chapter and verse. I reread it recently; it holds up just fine.

Stories about Tarzan worked pretty well for me for years till I discovered science fiction. Ray Bradbury's *The Martian Chronicles* and a lot of Robert Heinlein's work converted me into a full-fledged liberal, although *The Puppet Masters* gave me night sweats for a few weeks.

Christmas

Every Christmas we drove into The Little Town Nearby to see the lights, strings of bulbs, and greenery strung across the main streets. We actually found a place to park and sit to admire them. We appreciated simplicity in those days, but The Little Town Nearby had more visual treats to enjoy than anything in the country except the clouds and the vast sky. I don't think anyone decorated homes in the country.

One year the tune "Rudolph the Red-nosed Reindeer" became popular with some kids, but not me. I didn't like it then, and I don't like it now, nor do I like anyone who does like it. Or any citizen who ever did like it, for that matter. Too cute. Cute erodes intellect.

The Parents never quite explained Christmas to me, but I enjoyed it hugely. I still feel cheated by the toy shortage during World War Two, but I've tried to make up for it with Macintosh computers. The Mother forced me to bed early on Christmas Eve, allowing as how I could get up again if and when Santa arrived. The men then went outside and threw clods onto the roof; this electrified me as I pretended to be asleep, so I rose and reveled in whatever goodies I found under the tree. I treasured those Bild-A-Set weapons of mass destruction. Cast iron tractors and trucks became highly prized, but I didn't collect them; they disappeared into trash heaps somewhere. Back of the chicken house, I suspect.

All of this took place early enough for The Mother to haul me off to Midnight Mass at the Church in The Little Town Nearby. I knew it would be a long session, but it was the only time I got to stay up that late. Besides, several of the male parishioners had achieved a sort of bulletproof drunkenness by midnight, and I enjoyed watching them; it helped keep me awake.

In the fullness of time I learned that Santa Claus was only a myth perpetrated by The Parents. The entire country seemed to be in on it, though, and I began to wonder what other outright lies I had been subjected to. Church came to mind, as did quite a few of the things I had learned at The One-Room Country Grade School. I grew skeptical, approaching the foothills of cynicism.

The religion and the dynamite both seemed to me to prove that I could find more fun than hoeing weeds or stacking wood, as I suspected all along. But making a departure had to wait until later; in the meantime, I studied on how to avoid work, a skill I honed into razor sharpness.

But first I had to go to school.

CHAPTER FOUR

GRADE SCHOOL ON THE PRAIRIE, OR, erudition reduction ad absurdum

When and if a farm kid survived to the age of six years the State stepped in and required the little booger to attend grade school. Farm kids would attend a country grade school. We had such an institution, a mile from The Little House on the Prairie, Part Two, so the Mother drove me the first day of school. Afterwards I walked to school with some other social outcasts of similar ages, toting my lunch with me. The Parents assured me I would learn to read, so I agreed to give it a shot, but I didn't know any more about school than Jack the Ripper knew about foreplay.

Getting There

The Country Grade School lay directly across a section (a square mile) from our farm. At first I walked the two miles around the section with other kids headed for school. Later I could trudge straight across the section, which reduced the trek to one mile, but that meant no companions from whom to learn smutty stories.

I described all this to my son on his first day of grade school:

DAD: Boy, as a kid I had to walk two miles to school.

SON: Right. Uphill both ways.

DAD: Right. Naked.

SON: Right. With savages attacking you.

DAD: Right. Through cactus and boulders.

SON: Right. And blizzards.

DAD: Right.

Well, perhaps it wasn't all that bad, but it was a mile or two, and sometimes it rained, and sometimes it snowed, and sometimes one of The Parents would drive me over. The school didn't have any phones in it, either. Some of our Midwestern blizzards dropped so much snow on us that our automobiles couldn't cope, so a team of horses and a wagon would come to the rescue. I assumed some time or other we would have to over-night at the school, since we had plenty of fuel, but we never did. I thought I missed out on a considerable educational opportunity.

The Building

The Country Grade School rose up out of the prairie in 1885, making it three years older than The Father. The Brother attended The Country Grade School, the very same one, and survived. The School, built with limestone, featured a belfry on the front end, housing a bell I never heard ring, the pull rope for it having rotted away some time during the Spanish-American War. Heat came from a coal-burning stove, fueled from a coal shed adjacent to the far end of the building.

The Teacher ruled over us from a desk at the west end of the interior, facing a half dozen rows of desks of varying sizes.

The congregation consisted of grades one through eight; the bigger kids got the bigger desks.

The Country Grade School and assembled scholars, date unknown, but pretty early, since there's no merry-go-round or coal shed. The Teacher is unidentified, but my money is on the tall lady on the far right, back row.

The east or front end of the school had three small rooms: an entry in which the boys hung their coats and stashed their lunches, a "library" which contained a tattered set of the *World Book Encyclopedia* and a few children's books, and the girls' coat room, a Shangri-La rarely entered by boys, but serving as a handy place for girls to go cry. Perhaps eight feet square, these rooms seemed larger back then. Lots of things seemed smaller after I'd grown up. A matter of relativity once again, as I've explained to my relatives.

Outbuildings

Other than the coal shed, the outbuildings included a horse barn on the north side of the lot; many of the older boys rode horses to school; a few girls did. After the first few years of my education The Father would buy me ponies to ride to school. I came to realize eventually that he got them cheap because he selected psychological misfits, ponies not fit for cohabiting with human beings. One such beast would not under any circumstances cross a culvert, and there were eight or ten of them between the farm and The Country Grade School. Instead this pony stopped, bucked me off, and returned to the farm. I usually went back to the farm myself, crying and cursing as well as I knew how, vowing vengeance and kicking rocks. In time the horse quit bucking me off after I convinced the critter there existed far worse evils than crossing culverts. This did nothing for the pony's psychological state, but it did wonders for mine. The beast became something of an existentialist, long before either of us had heard the word. So did I.

So as I grew slowly into taking charge of myself, I began to modify my environment as much as I could, horses included.

The Country Grade School, like our house, had no electricity, no running water, and no gas. In both places we used a few coal-oil lanterns on dark days. We made do, as did most farm families, with outdoor facilities. At school we had a boys' toilet and a girls' toilet, crude but functional. No one ever tried to move them that I recall; concrete bases anchored them pretty firmly.

The grounds also contained a merry-go-round which we propelled to high speeds during recesses. If a boy slipped and fell off the device just right, he could often catch a glimpse up the skirts of the girls on the device, but The Teacher figured out that stunt and protected the little darlings. I didn't learn as much as I wanted to, but I did discover Dorothy wore panties made from feed sacks. Dorothy typified to us the most bewildering creature in all Christendom, a Big Girl, four or five grades ahead of us. She became a topic of considerable speculation by small fry. And by the big fry, too; the bigger the fry the more detailed the speculation.

A boy's toilet from another country one-room grade school. As I recall, ours was not quite so lavishly appointed. Courtesy of the Kansas Historical Society.

The Teacher

On the first day of school the sky darkened, the earth trembled, and The Teacher advanced on me, and I advanced on her. Little did I dream I would spend eight long grades writhing under the thumb of this corporeal catastrophe (she'd have dressed out at about 275, I reckoned). I never had a different teacher, not counting nuns, until I entered The High School. A strange policy, that, but the School Board had its own logic.

The Father served on the School Board; indeed, he chaired it for a time. He took credit for hiring The Teacher, and The Sister and I later argued with him long and hard, to no avail, that The Teacher couldn't teach a cow to go moo. She believed in rigorous drill and iron discipline for children. I suppose she meant well, but we all considered her a Nazi, very likely a storm trooper. Her ancestors were German, and we had a war going on with those guys. We didn't know about their concentration camps then, but we would have thought she could have run one efficiently. We suspected her of spying for the Third Reich, but never wondered what she might have had under surveillance. The horse barn, maybe. The older boys thought as a patriotic gesture someone should shoot her. I had no objection, but I had no gun then, either.

The Fat Kid

One memorable day The Fat Kid tested The Teacher's authority. The Teacher declared recess had ended. That did not sit well with The Fat Kid, a first-grader who, like me, had been spoiled rotten. So The Fat Kid decided to spend the day playing outside. He responded to The Teacher's command to return to class by throwing himself headlong onto the ground, screaming and kicking and tearing up tufts of grass with both fists. The rest of us watched, admittedly impressed, but The Porcine Pedagogue, with a two hundred and fifty-pound weight advantage on The Fat Kid, simply dropped on him like the wages of sin.

We heard flatulent, strangled sobs blubbering out from beneath The Teacher. When The Fat Kid finally burrowed his way out into the light and the air, purple-faced and sucking wind, seeking only truth, justice, and the American Way, he contained not a smidgen of rebellion, nor would he as long as he remained at The Country Grade School. You could have run a divining rod over him and not found an atom of anarchy. The rest of us entered these happenings into our data banks.

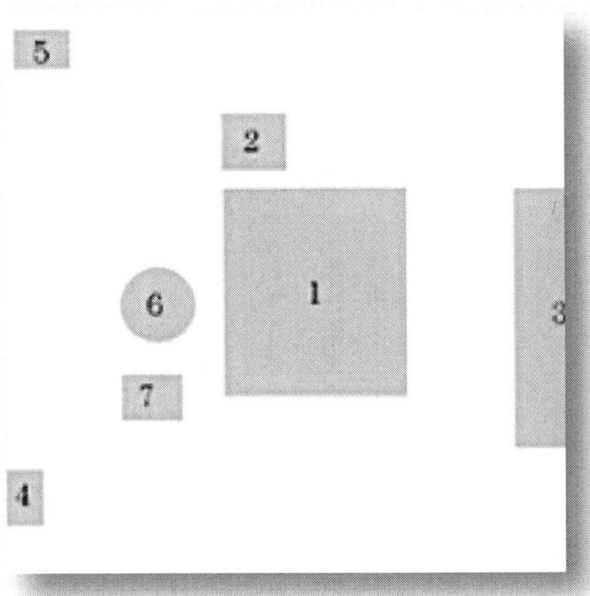

Map of the Country Grade School yard: 1 is the school house itself, 2 the coal shed, 3 the horse barn, 4 the boys' toilet, 5 the girls' toilet, 6 the merry-go-round, and 7 the water pump. Plan created by the author.

That Fat Kid developed into a sort of all-purpose putz. A few years later we amused ourselves by crawling through a culvert under the lane leading into the schoolyard. It came The Fat Kid's turn, and, being a fat kid, he had more trouble than us skinny guys (sigh) getting through the corrugated steel pipe. He got perhaps three-quarters of the way when we began to throw clods and rocks at the ends of the culvert, while screaming

"Tornado!" "Run for your lives!" and, I modestly suggest, a masterpiece of improvisation: "Flash flood! Flash flood!" It hadn't rained in months, but The Fat Kid forgot that.

He shot out of the culvert like a Nike rocket, and we never got him in there again. He was never meant to be a farmer, and I could sympathize with that. I later heard he became an art major.

Programs of Study

The Country Grade School offered a curriculum of extreme simplicity. Since The Teacher had to deal with eight grades simultaneously, she needed to keep seven classes busy while she heard the eighth group recite. My grade contained only three students; I don't think any class had more; the total head count for all eight grades usually numbered around a dozen or so.

We got lots of reading assignments after we learned to read, which suited me just fine. I had muttered darkly after coming home from the first day of school that I had not yet learned to read and might not bother to go back. But we sucked up reading skills by means of forced drill with flash cards. These cards came in kits that someone sold to teachers. I watched the cards grow old in the service over the years, increasingly yellow and brittle.

But we endured the adventures of Dick and Jane and their weak-minded dog, Spot. None of them looked like anyone we knew, though.

Part of our reading drills demanded recitation from a list of words in a primer. Once I looked ahead, finding to my horror the word "Nanny" lurking about fifty words ahead. This would have caused no alarm for most kids, but in our family we used the word "nanny" as a euphemism for excrement. One made nanny, for example. I didn't want to say the word aloud in class, of course, but there it was. And as I calculated the words the other kiddy scholars would say I became convinced that my time was running short, perhaps only a few days. I supposed I would be beaten to death by the elders, who would then leave my corpse rotting out on the prairie like a buffalo. I'd never seen a buffalo, of course, and didn't know they were actually bison, but that's what I supposed.

The interior of a typical country grade school; not mine, but the spitting image of the one I attended. Photograph by the author.

The day arrived. We read words, and "Nanny" appeared on my list. I sort of mumbled it, fully expecting to have the nanny beaten out of me and to be exiled onto the prairie. Someone would surely tell The Mother after they'd lashed me with a barbed wire flail. Who knew that girls might have Nanny for a name? I didn't know any named that, for Pete's sake.

No one cared a rat's rectum, one way or the other, and life went on. I gave thanks and considered the advantages of meeting adversity head on.

Later I began to wonder about the origins of such a slang term. No slang dictionary in my library had any more than "nanny-goat," and the Oxford English Dictionary could only add "nanny-horse." I guess we were breaking fresh ground in those days. What a pity no one knew about it.

The Teacher hammered mathematics into us the same way; we recited over and over until a store dummy could have learned the multiplication tables, even if our resident bully couldn't. Eighth-graders might frolic in algebraic foothills, but the rest of us drilled on what a fifty-cent calculator can do today, the utter basics. When The Teacher called on us to recite our "times tables," if we hesitated she would accuse us of "counting up," a mortal sin for little kiddies, implying we'd used our fingers to calculate sums under ten. The Teacher accused me several times of cheating, which I wasn't, but we had no court of appeal.

One evening at The Little House on the Prairie, Part Two, lying on the floor with a Big Chief tablet and a No. 2 pencil, I faced the dilemma of just how to make an eight. The Teacher taught numbers to us using weird verbal descriptions; a number one, for example, was a "big tall Indian chief." It sort of worked, but the eight defeated me; the description was "wiggly worm, back home, eight." This kind of monkey talk stupefied me.

On that glorious evening, however, I made a wiggly worm, the letter "s," my initial, after all. An epiphany struck, and I connected the lower end of the s with the upper end—

behold! An eight! I've never had much trouble making eights since. Some, not much.

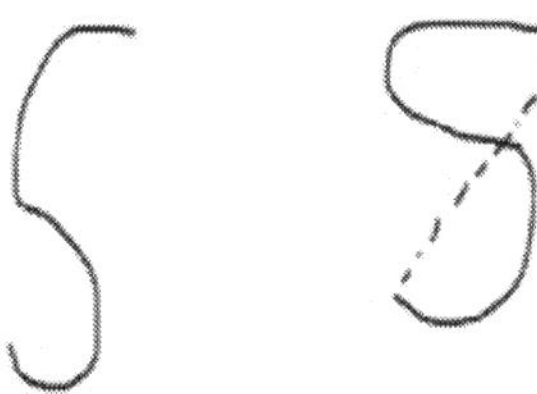

Wiggly-worm, back home, eight! Child's play. Graphic by the author, if you can believe it.

Geography (which we learned to spell with the mnemonic device, "George Eliot's old grandfather rode a pig home yesterday,") tested our memory, but introduced us to worlds of which we had never dreamed. The ancient Greeks seemed like fun guys, and the Romans even more, an attitude no doubt colored by the Church. All this took place during World War Two, so we concerned ourselves mostly with the dirty Nazis and the filthy Japs. I'm not sure any of us knew Italy took any part in the war, or even that such a place as Italy existed. I think we thought that Rome was a country by itself.

Over the years, though, I grew to wonder and worry about George Eliot's old grandfather and exactly what condition he got into to decide to ride a pig home. How much homemade bust-head did he have to imbibe? Did the pig have an opinion on all this? For that matter, who waited for gramps at home, and how did they greet the old man's arrival? What happened to the pig? I've never met anyone named George Eliot, but if I ever do I'm ready with my questions.

In college I rode home in a police car once or twice, but never on a pig. I wonder if Gramps rode sidesaddle. But where would you find a saddle that fit a pig?

My Fellow Scholars

My classmates included a terminally shy boy who became The Best Friend and an apprentice nymphomaniac, The Bad Little Girl, who amused the boys at recess by showing them her panties with her in them. The Bad Little Girl performed this cunning stunt in the schoolyard, out of sight of the teacher and the other scholars. Then she would lead the other girls into the horse barn and do something else, barring the boys. We lacked the nerve to peek through the cracks and knotholes, I guess, the more fools we.

Neither classmate comprised any intellectual threat, so I resorted to the "library" and *The World Book*, a multi-volume encyclopedia at the kiddy level. Still, with not much else to do, I, like The Brother before me, tied into it and waded through the entire set.

In *The World Book* I read about dinosaurs and how some of the larger ones had two brains, a small one in their head and an even smaller one in their hind end to guide that part of their massive bodies. I explained this to The Bully, a mouth-breather who got to the eighth grade without learning to read beyond the third. I then proposed that he was probably built the same way; a small brain in his head (I still wish I'd known the word "ganglia" then) and another in his butt to keep it tracking behind him. As he usually did when confused or irritated by smaller fry, The Bully charged, but I easily outran him. For that matter the coal shed could outrun him.

The Bully had it tough in school; The Teacher hammered away at him with numbers and words, but with little impact. The Bully's only claim to fame, besides sheer heft, was that he rode a Palomino horse to school, a notoriously thin-skinned breed. After mid-afternoon liberation from school, The Bully climbed on his horse and raced around the school a couple of times, scattering young 'uns in all directions. I marvel he never killed any of us.

A family photo of me driving my horse to school with The Best Friend riding behind me. I had, it would seem, just been promoted to the rank of Sergeant. The Mother named this horse Boots, which I despised as too cute, four white feet or not. Cute, I sensed, diluted masculinity. I still think so. From the author's collection.

But though small in stature, we younger kids enjoyed numerical superiority. Since The Bully, like the rest of us boys, left his lunch in the cloakroom until noon, rarely did a day go by without one of us announcing a call of nature, which necessitated leaving the building. On the way back through the cloakroom we often found The Bully's lunch bucket and made a deposit therein, frequently a horse dumpling. His responses pretty much gratified us, and he enlivened recesses for us considerably. He should have lost weight chasing us around.

We deduced that while God definitely had not created all men equal, we had equalizers. The Bully had a lazy habit of leaving the saddle on his horse all day, in keeping with his nature. The fields around the school contained cockleburs along the fences. A cocklebur grows a flower bud with lots of thorny spines on it, about the size of a thumb.

Cockleburs, just as bad as they looked. They grew wild all around the schoolyard. Indeed, they grew all over the county and probably the state. Perhaps the entire Midwest. Noxious weeds, to be sure, but useful for punishing bullies. From the author's collection.

A few of these, properly placed, would cause the Palomino to buck The Bully straight up into the rafters, or on a good day, the roof. I expect these experiences further diluted his enjoyment of lower education. Hey, he had his problems; we had ours. When I heard in church that the Lord had said, "Vengeance is mine," I found the concept astonishing. My mates and I managed our own vengeances for years, with cockleburs and horse apples aplenty to serve us. Heaven helps those who help themselves, sure enough. That was one thing I learned in Sunday School. That was about it, though.

Recesses, or The Efficacy of Prayer

It's a terrible death to be taught to death, so we rejoiced in midmorning and midafternoon recesses. Most recesses offered at least a modicum of mindless fun, and they beat the everlasting hell out of class time. We played a variety of games. Sometimes we dug out a softball bat and ball and played "move-up," a game in which The Teacher pitched, and the students rotated around the field. We started in left field and "moved up" until we got up to bat again. That meant quite a few peewees meandered around the field at any moment making it difficult to hit a grounder without nailing one of them.

Almost no kid could catch the ball off the bat; instead they dived, ran, jumped out of the way. One memorable day I dropped a soft fly into left field, and Allah Be Praised! it went over the privacy screen and into the girls' toilet. The Bully, playing outfield, lumbered in after the ball; there ensued squealing, screams, and thuds. The Teacher suspected that's what I had in mind all along, but she couldn't prove it. I didn't have that much bat control, anyway, since I didn't know what it was.

The Teacher supervised another of our favorite games, "Ante-Over," using the same mushy softball. Also known as Eenie Einie, Auntie Over, Andy Over, Anti-Over, Annie I Over, Ante-I-over, Annie Annie Over, Annie Over the Shanty, and a few other local variations, according to slang source books.

Half the students gathered on one side of the school; the other half deployed to the other side. A big kid would hurl the ball over the schoolhouse, and if the other side missed catching it, they threw it back. If by some fluke someone caught it, that kid gave the ball to his leader and they all took off for the other side, whereupon the scholars there raced around the other end of the building to escape them. Anyone the leader could hit with the ball had to play on his side for the rest of the game.

A simple game, to be sure, but strategies emerged. I once sent half our group around one end of the school and the other half around the other, causing mass confusion among the enemy. The Teacher declared my plan a travesty; she would have branded me a Communist, had she known about Communists.

Every so often some wily little rascal would substitute a horse apple for the softball and hurl it over the school. That caused trouble on the other side, especially if someone caught it.

Oddly enough, we didn't play "Hide and Seek" very often. We had about a half-acre to frolic around in, and recesses lasted long enough for the game. Occasionally we played it just for a change of pace.

The devil of temptation came to me once and after seeing the guy playing "It" to his base, counting to one hundred, I went home. I considered this a masterstroke of evasion, but The Teacher did not; she took me aside and spoke to me next time she saw me. So did The Mother. I had to go back.

In the winter The Teacher might keep us inside if the weather grew too cold for fun and games. But somehow we knew some games we could play in the snow, and play them we did. I guess the older kids taught the younger kids these games, generation after generation. But how they started would make a good doctoral dissertation, if it hasn't already. I'd look it up if I cared a lot more about it, but I don't. Meaner kids, often the river rats, made special snowballs for pelting the rest of us. Their snowballs were either solid ice or had a stone in the middle. In either case they hurt, a whole lot.

Other Games

We enjoyed acting out our favorite radio or movie stories. After deciding who was to play The Lone Ranger, we raced around the schoolyard on our imaginations, as only small boys and Monty Pythons can do.

Most boys, left to themselves, invented games involving guns, the simplest of which was called just that: "Guns." If a shingle blew off the roof of the horse barn or the school, it barely settled to the ground before one of us snatched it up and carved it into the shape of some firearm or other. This sustained us for months at a time; rampant slaughters ensued, even if no one wanted to perform as any of the Axis powers.

One day One-Eyed John brought a real gun to school, a .22 revolver, and a pocket full of ammunition. At the morning recess while the rest of us played softball, One-Eyed John went to the boys' toilet, and while enthroned therein shot out all the knotholes from the inside. When he finally stepped out, he found his fellow scholars huddled behind the merry-go-round, the pump, the girls' toilet, and quite a crowd of us clustered behind The Teacher. The Teacher confiscated the pistol. I wanted it, but I didn't get it.

We tried to play better known games, even if we didn't know how. If The Teacher did, she didn't let on.

Somehow the school had obtained a few rudimentary sports objects: a softball and bat, which we sort of understood, but also a football, a basketball, and a goal for the basketball.

We deduced we should throw the basketball into the hoop, the cords from which had disappeared several generations earlier. But basketball doesn't have much appeal for people four feet tall. As for the football, we pumped it up with a hand pump and tried to kick it to death. You have to understand our total football experience came from watching a few seconds of bowl game newsreels once a year. We didn't have the foggiest as to what it was all about; I doubt any one of us knew about four downs or laterals or a drag bunt or a PAT or any of it.

Of course, in grade school little boys got together and told dirty jokes. Slightly hampered by not knowing any, we did the best we could. I can only remember one story from those days, not worth repeating; let it sink into well-deserved obscurity. It would only have disappointed you, anyway. Trust me.

Let's put it this way, the most successful jokes for us were faux book titles, such as *Yellow Mississippi* by I. P. Freely, or *Tiger's Revenge* by Claude Balls, and the one and only *Hole in the Bed* by Mr. Completely. We made do with what we had. *The Castrated Chinaman* by Spade Cooley won favor, too; Spade Cooley headed up a Western swing band.

One budding genius found some amusement in filling his lunch bucket with rocks, tying a rope to its handle, and standing on the coal shed roof whirling it in a large vertical circle. What could happen did; another kid ran around a corner and into the orbit of the lunch pail, which nailed him right between the eyes, laying him out. He survived but carried a scar to remind him not to race around corners without checking first.

Some found amusement in fighting. Not each other very often, but annually the parents hauled us off to another country grade school somewhere for smallpox vaccinations. This health measure took most of a morning. While the girls squealed and got their shots, the boys gathered in the horse barn. Sooner or later somebody offered some sass to somebody else, and the fight was on. A couple of the boys from rival institutions rolled around in the horse hockey till adults came, pulled them apart, then took them aside and spoke to them.

Some fink in my school spied on me and ratted me out whenever I tried to get extra cute. I would execute some nastiness or other, but then I would find myself being lined out by one of The Parents, quoting me verbatim. That slowed me down some, but I never deduced who did the ratting. I have pondered over the years and have settled on three suspects, The Bully, The Fat Kid, and the Best Friend. I've lost track of all three, so I forgive them.

Deviations from the Norm, Curriculum-wise

Meanwhile the school program seemed bent on robbing us of our manhood even before we really had any. The books we read all had happy endings, and once a week we were forced to sing songs, an experience I found repulsive. I never could sing and I never expect to, for which I blame the harridan who came around weekly to force us to croak out melodies. She especially grooved on "Juanita," a pseudo-Mexican song of love and such, which she banged out on an old upright piano that hadn't been tuned since The Roaring Twenties. I detested "Juanita" at the time; I still do, and I always will, and I will have no truck with anyone who doesn't also hate it. Go to the iTunes music store and look up Jim Reeves, if you just must hear it. I still say, "double puke!" For that matter, "triple puke!"

We had just begun to endure another music lesson one day when a knock came at the door. The Teacher answered and found a young stud Highway Patrolman offering to show the students his car and equipment, including his GUNS. Our teacher realized that the boys would erupt into full-scale rioting if she sent him away, so we got to examine the trooper's shootin' irons. He had a twelve-gauge shotgun loaded with double-aught shot (.33" in diameter) and guns that shot tear gas, and such. I expect the trooper really wanted to impress upon us up-and-coming felons what we would face in later life; for some of us it worked. And we didn't have to sing about "'Nita, Juanita" and softly flowing fountains or such abominations. The music teacher sneaked away, badly bested; when she returned, we paid even less attention to her. Making a living in the arts is hard cheese for anyone, especially in education.

That Country Grade School had its share of dangers, though. Once I burst out the door for recess, ready to rumble, but I tripped and fell headlong into a pile of cinders. One of them sliced an inch-long gash under my left eye, so deep that The Teacher took me home. The Mother panicked and took me to town to the family physician who stitched me up. But the swine neglected to clean out the wound before sewing it up, so I sport a blue scar from the coal dust under my eye, and I have had it ever since. The only cure for it would be cremation or some sort of facial amputation or transplant.

Twice a year, once for Christmas, once for The Great Bust Out every spring, The Country Grade School produced a sort of feeble-minded variety show. Parents would come and beam proudly at their progeny as we demonstrated what complete horses' asses could be made of us with even minimal direction. The Teacher hung a tatty old curtain at the front of the room; we rehearsed skits of the sort that required no royalty fees. The entire student body formed the Rhythm Band after The Teacher handed out various percussive devices. While she took the melody on piano, we all wailed away on drums, wooden sticks, tambourines, etc. I had the only triangle in the group and stepped out rather briskly, I thought, when we played "The

Bells of St. Mary's," another dumb song, but better than "Juanita."

> *ASIDE: As I write this a fantasy has just come to me—let's reassemble the Rhythm Band for a long-delayed encore performance. Our audiences have all passed away; many of the performers are dead or in rest homes or penitentiaries, but we could reassemble those left and bring a certain maturity to "The Bells of St Mary's." If you were one of the happy players, get in touch with me; we'll give it a go. If we can find more than four survivors, we're talking CDs.*

We had to learn the lines to mindless skits. I don't know that anyone ever learned them all, but we were young and did what we could in a few rehearsals. I couldn't do it now. Such merry pranks punctuated my eight grades in seven years. The Teacher thought I could handle second and third grade together—let's face it, one of those dung-slinging chimpanzees back in Chapter Two could have done it—so I took those two grades in one year. Did The Father serving as chairman of the school board have anything to do with that? I'm the last to say so, but this educational jump-start put me a year ahead of my classmates, or made me a year younger than my classmates, depending on how you look at it. The Teacher did me no favor socially; I didn't get back in sync until I flunked out of college.

I don't know how long The Teacher continued in her position. She married while I attended The Country Grade School, leading to speculation by the older boys about the honeymoon, as verbalized in

"The ground was plowed for miles around,
Where her big fat ass had hit the ground."

We'd never heard of Noel Coward at that point, but we loved sophisticated humor, nonetheless.

Thus I learned to read and write, to cipher a bit, and to get out of The Country Grade School, the Andersonville of primary education, and thus entered that Land of Oz, The High School in The Little Town Nearby. I entered it as a farm kid suddenly thrust among the sophisticates, degenerates, and high livers of big city life. Lots of novelties, like girls, lay, to coin a phrase, in wait for me. But those stories have to wait for another day and another chapter.

In the meantime The Parents had an assortment of tasks for me to execute before I made any sort of getaway.

I soldiered on.

CHAPTER FIVE

FARM WORK, AND THE AVOIDANCE THEREOF, OR, BLOOD, SWEAT, AND BULLSHIT

I cannot imagine why, but some of my kinfolk recently urged me to read a book by a guy who grew up on an Iowa farm. The author described his childhood, including all the chores his father assigned him. A few chapters into this volume I realized—angels and ministers of grace defend us!—that this guy actually did all those jobs, willingly, and even tried to do them well. Then he hunted around to find more to do.

I find such actions incomprehensible; I had difficulty grasping such foolishness. For years I busted my hump trying to avoid work as much as possible, with tolerable success. I worried early on that The Parents might actually work me to death if I didn't take evasive action. If I sensed any work on my immediate horizon, I would ease on out the back door and run the bottoms for a while.

My life in agriculture took place on two farms, the first being The Little House on the Prairie, Part Two, as described earlier. The Father rented this place during the Depression, and he took pride in making every payment on time. He eventually bought 160 acres just a quarter mile to the north, that being The Little House on the Prairie, Part Three.

According to family legend, the previous owner married a tubercular divorcee with several kids. She died a few years after the marriage, and her widower ran off the road and over a bluff in Colorado with fatal results.

Conditions

Conditions on our little farm lacked much sophistication; I had to learn to read by lamps burning kerosene.

The sort of kerosene lamps used by farm folk before the installation of electricity. Photo by the author.

These lamps gave off dim light but also considerable heat; the pleasures of reading thus came at a price. Such devices resembled bombs waiting to go off; they would have served admirably as Molotov cocktails, but farm kids had never heard of such a thing.

We had a radio powered by a car battery in the early days. When the battery grew weak and the signals began to fade, The Father hauled the battery into town to get it recharged. This scheme worked, the only problem being the inevitable spilling of battery acid while carrying it around; that acid ate holes in anything, especially rugs and small boys. With no electricity or gas The Mother cooked on a large wood- burning range, a black, cast-iron monster in the kitchen.

A wood-burning cook stove similar to the behemoth we had in our kitchen. Photo by the author.

Part of my standing orders and The Brother's before me required keeping the wood box full. The Father cut down trees or found downed timber, then sawed it up and brought the logs to the woodpile not far from the kitchen door. He cut and collected lots of timber along the creek trickling across our farm. We hooked up a buzz saw of melodramatic dimensions and fed the wood to it. We gained as a result large stacks of firewood and a hell of a pile of sawdust. I don't recall that we did anything with the sawdust, but the firewood kept us alive.

Burning wood creates ashes, which in our stove fell into a tray below the main combustion chamber. To remove the ashes The Father opened a small door, slid out the tray full of ashes and possibly glowing embers, and removed it for disposal. He arose early every winter morning and removed the ashes and then built another fire. Alas, he might spill a few ashes on the rug as he took the tray outdoors, causing The Mother to go ballistic and tell him to just leave it alone; she'd do it herself. He affably agreed, and I don't believe he ever carried another ash. I studied this ploy carefully. I doubt The Father ever realized he changed my life with that little stunt; over the years the usefulness of that logic has never weakened nor left me. I thank him to this day; he saved me from a mountain of useless labor, even if he didn't quite feel the same way about farm work, like hoeing potatoes or castrating calves.

Horehound

Now, a farm is a patch of real estate just overflowing with work; I figured that out early on. When we moved to The Little House on the Prairie, Part Three, The Mother observed that the knoll on which we planned to live was covered with a weed called horehound, a.k.a. *Marrubium vulgare*.

I never asked why they called it horehound; even then I suspected I would get one of The Mother's snaky left jabs if I brought up such a topic as hores. It just wouldn't do to have it all over the place, so The Mother decided I had to pull it all up, load it into my little red wagon, and haul it off somewhere to be burned. My heart sank as I surveyed this sea of horehound. This job I just couldn't escape, so for a couple of months— maybe a little less than that—I pulled, piled, and hauled.

The only potential fun in the whole sordid business would come when I burned it, but the grownups reserved that entertainment for themselves; I merely supplied the fodder. Eventually I whipped the horehound into submission, but a stray plant would pop up now and again. I would nail it and eliminate it from our hill, lest it spread. It's such nasty stuff that a cow won't eat it, and if the cow was fool enough to eat some, then you can't eat the cow or drink her tainted milk for some little while. I never determined the half-life of horehound. My last visit to that farm, sixty years after I had cleared it of horehound, I find it coming back. Truly, nature persists and wins in the end. But I'm not pulling up any more *Marrubium vulgare* unless it's on land I have personally homesteaded.

Horehound, a wretched weed that had "taken" the hill on which we sought to live. From the author's collection.

Since I imagine any future homesteading will have to happen on Mars, it doesn't seem too likely. Nor do I like to think about what kind of horehound grows on the Red Planet. It might devour me. Perhaps I had just read too much pulp science fiction, but I don't regret a bit of it.

Critters

Pets helped entertain us a bit, but The Mother allowed no beast of any sort into the house unless sick or needing tending, such as a calf or baby chickens. We always had a dog or two, conglomerate breeds dumped in the country by city people. We all loved a superlative farm dog called Flops in honor of his ears, but an ignorant son of a bitch of a farmer ran into him with his mowing machine, mangling him badly. The Brother had to take his .22 rifle and dispatch Flops; it caused us all considerable anguish. I proposed shooting the mouth-breathing moron on the mower, and I think the proposal received some serious consideration.

Cats prowled around the barn, but not house cats; not even yard cats, but feral cats. I liked cats; they seemed cool before cool became cool, and they devoured mice to earn their pay.

Calves seemed cute enough to be pets, but we all liked hamburger too much to grow fond of them.

We loathed pigs as filthy beasts, but we endured them because of the sausage The Bohemian Mother and Aunt created. Truly God-given delights. Bohemian gods, to be sure, but that sausage would have converted Genghis Kahn to be born again to Christianity.

Once a year we butchered a hog or two. The men dispatched the porker, hung it up, disemboweled it, and carved it into manageable chunks. Often the children grabbed the hog bladder to kick around during this abattoir like miniature soccer players. Eventually the bladder burst, and some carnivore would snack on it.

During this frivolity the women stuffed hog meat into a grinder and processed the results into sausage, which was the point in the first place. They would seal that meat into glass jars and shelve them for other days. When the blizzards struck and the mercury dropped, sausage and biscuits enabled a guy to attack the jobs for the day, no matter what had to be done.

The Father once bought a prize boar hog with the ostentatious name of W. L. Means III. For years I treasured a photo of him from a farm newspaper, a rear view, featuring a scrotum Zeus himself would have been happy to drag around Olympus. W.L. didn't do much but loll around in the shade, then get up when the season came and service all the lady pigs. Afterward he collapsed back into boar lethargy and dreamed boar dreams. Farmers used the euphemism "service." Kids did not.

The Father assigned me a daily hike of about a mile west into one of our pastures to water the cattle there. He had installed a gasoline engine to pump water into a stock tank. I found this task easy enough, and since I had to turn the engine off when the tank got full, I could loll in the shade and consider my future, sexual and otherwise.

I always took along my trusty .22. That made me very happy indeed when I encountered a tarantula skittering across the pasture. Having heard those nasty devils could jump impressive distances, I pumped a few slugs into him to slow him down. I grew in time to consider all life sacred, except spiders.

I'd occasionally meet a snake out on the prairie, and depending upon the type it was, I would dispatch it or let it go. I had no qualms about dispatching copperheads, nor would I now. They kill people, as well as animals. Other venomous snakes included water moccasins (cottonmouths) who hung around the creek. Supposedly we had a plethora of rattlesnakes around. I have yet to see a rattlesnake in the wild, only in zoos and such. I've even hunted them, without success.

When an animal of ours died it would have taken weeks to dig it a grave you could stuff a cow into, so The Father called "The Dead Wagon." A man would appear equipped to haul the carcass away. I never knew what he did with the bodies; dumped them in a landfill, I suppose. I hope he didn't know any butchers.

We rarely bought any meat; we rented a very cold locker in town. When we butchered a calf, our butcher would cut and wrap the meat, then store it in the locker. We'd go get some when we needed it, and it would be frozen as hard as a rock, literally. Like you could drive nails with it, if you were so inclined. The Mother would thaw it out for a few days, then fry the living hell out of it and serve it. We all gobbled it down like good fellows and praised her for preparing it for us.

The Mother and the Chickens

The Mother did a big business in fowls. During the Depression we always ate well; after all, we lived where the food came from. Her fried chicken could have set chicken-frying records and won prizes had she entered them in the State Fair, but she never did. She never used a recipe, just heated a black cast iron skillet to near-incandescence, rolled chicken body parts in flour, and dropped them in. The pieces almost jumped out, but when they came to rest they became my favorite food—at least the white meat, and I devised ways of getting the wishbone, often succeeding. I had by then grown far too hip to crawl under the table and bawl for what I wanted.

A farm wife feeding her chickens. Not The Mother, but much like her. Courtesy Missouri Historical Society.

Kids grow up thinking their mother's cooking defined quality in food, but then that's all they know, so of course they would. In my case the evidence supported that position, about eighty percent of the time.

The Mother and The Aunt spent lots of time canning foodstuffs: sausage, corn, tomatoes, and such. Potatoes they kept in a sack in the cellar, as they did onions, but some stuff required preservation. The women acquired an adequate stock of Mason jars, the kind with metal lids that screwed on over a red rubber gasket. They prepared the food, then sealed it in the jars and stored it away for the winter. Occasionally a jar exploded, but not very often. The canned sausage looked about as nasty as anything you'd care to see, white and gelatinous, but when heated, became a food for the gods. We lacked quite a bit from being gods, but then we had all those canned goods, and no gods showed up to contest us, and racoons and possums couldn't get in the house, so we scarfed up the goodies.

The Grandmother had raised her daughters in the Bohemian traditions, so when they put up jams and jellies the good times began to roll. Their strawberry jam made life worth living; put on a hot biscuit for breakfast it prepared you to face the day. I didn't deserve such delicacies, of course, but that never kept me from getting them.

However, one lives and possibly learns. The Mother's method of preparing beefsteak consisted of hammering it into flaccidity, rolling it in flour, and frying the bejazuz out of it. Think chicken-fried steak, only crisper. But in college I encountered a broiled steak in an all-night diner and swore great oaths, thinking of roads not taken. The chicken eggs we sold or bartered in town. Eggs sold for sixty cents a dozen then, a factoid explained to me with some vigor when I tripped over a rock and smashed an entire basket of them. I was immediately taken aside and spoken to.

The Mother usually assigned me to gather eggs, which involved reaching under the chickens roosting in compartments three or four rows high.

A chicken roost, with a nest of straw in each compartment. One tried to reach under the chicken and harvest the eggs without offending her. Not always possible. From the author's collection.

A pedestrian job at best, livened up considerably when a chicken objected to molestation and pecked a hole in my hand, or when I found no eggs under the chicken but a bulging, belching blacksnake instead. Blacksnakes liked eggs and preferred to eliminate the middleman, going directly to the source. The Mother came upon a blacksnake once while gathering eggs, screamed bloody murder, dragged the snake out of the nest, snatched up a hatchet, and turned him (or her) into blacksnake filets. No piece over a few inches long survived, so the chickens ate the snake. Few people think of chickens as carnivores, but sometimes they turn cannibal.

I still don't like eggs very much. Never have. Never will. I know too much.

Wild Animals on the Farm

Local wild critters—rabbits and squirrels—became fair game when I began shooting. Raccoons and possums made regular night raids on our chicken house. When we heard the uproar The Father took a flashlight in one hand and a twelve-gauge shotgun in the other to defend our feathered commodities. He frequently did as much or more damage to the chickens than the intruders. I suggested to him once that he tape his flashlight to the shotgun barrel so he could aim with the pool of light. He looked at me strangely, but he didn't do it. I insist it would have worked, and come to think of it, I still have that shotgun. But I don't have a chicken house these days. Never have. Never will.

More serious predators preyed on our living assets, coyotes. I heard them yipping and yowling at night as I tried to sleep. I considered their musical output just lovely, but I haven't heard it in years now. Ranked near the bottom of the animal social scale, a coyote was a scraggly, filthy beast, a scavenger at best, rightfully considered a predator. After reading about big game hunting and safaris in Africa I decided to tie half a brick to a chicken, heave both fowl and brick over a twenty-foot bluff, then lie in wait for a coyote to come get the chicken, at which point I would nail it with my trusty .22 rifle. I never executed this plan, though. Thinking back on it, the plan contained flaws; the chicken and brick would have had my scent on them, which would have spooked the coyote into leaving the county. Well, the township at least.

But with a bounty of ten dollars each for coyotes, I could have retired early, without having to study foreign languages.

At one point The Father and I fenced the cattle and sheep pasture with woven wire to keep coyotes out. It worked just as The Father planned; no coyote got into that pasture. Unfortunately, however, we had fenced three coyotes in, and they had to be dispatched.

About that time somebody invented a gas gun, a sort of metal stake one could drive into the ground in coyote territory, cock it, and sprinkle *essense de femme coyote* on a rag tied to it. When a coyote came up to chew on the rag it shot a .38 cartridge filled with cyanide into the predator's face. Cruel, yes, but a farmer had to fight the environment to make a living for himself and his family. I think the mountain men used the same excuse about Indians. It was war, sure enough. If you'd ever seen what a coyote or two can do to a calf or a flock of lambs you'd understand why we killed them.

So the gas guns solved the coyote problem, pretty much, but then the field mice ate about everything farmers tried to grow. As they say, it isn't nice to fool Mother Nature. Gas guns disappeared.

Milking

I take some misbegotten pride in never having learned to milk a cow. That's where we got milk in those days, from cows. We'd never heard of pasteurization. The Father or The Brother put the cows in stalls early in the morning and in the evening to milk them, collecting the juice in galvanized buckets. They took the full buckets to the house for our use or emptied them into a cream can, a metal container holding about five gallons. The Father then sold the milk to grocery stores, sometimes bartering it for other foodstuffs.

It follows that farm kids learned quite early to milk cows; it's not all that much of a trick, really, and mostly the cows didn't seem to mind. But somehow I never got around to acquiring this skill. About the time I got old enough to do that job, The Brother took on the task to help earn college money. This arrangement suited me just fine. I would fool around the barn, finding new and interesting ways to get into trouble or hurt myself while The Brother did the milking.

The Brother once amused himself by squirting milk in my face when I got near enough to him. He could tweak a bovine nipple at an angle and hit me up to ten feet away with a stream of warm milk. I found this demeaning. I left for a little while, then found a three-foot length of two-by-four lumber and began sneaking up on The Brother from behind. As I recall, I intended to whomp a large knot on his head-bone as he milked. The Father intervened by lifting the two-by-four out of my hands just before I struck. So I didn't beat a bump on his skull, which makes me happy now, but he stopped squirting milk at me, which made me happy then.

The Father

The Father did almost all of the real work, of course; he farmed. He milked the cattle morning and evening till The Brother took over that chore, but all those cow-brutes, as The Father called them, had to be fed. He worked hard making the land capable of raising crops, then growing and managing the crops, and then harvesting and storing or selling the bounty.

Besides hogs and sheep we even owned guineas for a few years. Now you tell me how stupid a turkey is, and I agree; they'll drown in a rainstorm by looking up to see whence comes the water. But a turkey is a Harvard physics professor compared to a guinea. Also guineas make a god-awful noise when roused up, kind of like "pod-rack." Even The Mother couldn't stand them more than a couple of years. I don't recall that we ever ate one, anyway. I don't know what plans The Mother might have had for the guineas. I guess it was one of her failed experiments.

If The Father needed a small boy to fill in a gap in the labor force and I hadn't foreseen the work sufficiently to escape to some far corner of the farm, he would press me into service. I think he felt if I ate any of the food he produced I should help raise it. I had to agree.

I think The Father found farming a satisfactory way of life. No, he didn't burst out the door every morning yelling "Hay! Oats! Alfalfa! Cow-brutes!" but he didn't seem to seek any other way of life. I did, though. So did The Brother.

We had to move cattle from one pasture to another every now and then. I could pretend to be a cowboy, riding the range. If a car full of townies came along I imitated the Marlboro Man even before the admen had created him. But I soon realized that a cow-brute represented a level of stupidity I would not encounter again until I met The Bully in grade school. Cows seem huge when you're a little kid, but they also personify stupid; that's an essential part of being a cow. They had about the same IQ as a guinea.

Once The Father wanted to move about twenty cattle up a lane to a gravel road leading to another pasture. He wanted me to turn them north when they reached the gravel, so The Father stationed me to the south to head them. The cattle looked past me at a nearby pond; a great thirst came upon them, and so they mowed me down like a corn sheller and sauntered on over to the pond. The Father berated me for not stopping them. I argued that I could have stopped them if I'd had a gun, then I decided not to say anything more about it.

Sometimes The Father needed to take cattle to a metropolitan stockyard to sell them. I think he got a better price if he brought them himself. He and a neighbor or two would get them into a literal cattle car and ride with them all the way, then ride back in coaches like civilized human beings. The stockyards were about two hundred and fifty miles away, so I suppose they slept in the seats. I don't know if they even had compartments in those days, but they would have been pricey, anyway,

The Rancher

Father used to collaborate on these trips with The Rancher, a man adored by the local small boys for his profanity. For The Rancher profanity constituted not so much a weakness as a gift.

"That thing's pretty smelly, isn't it, Rancher?"

"Why, it'd stink a buzzard off a gut wagon a hundred yards away!"

When an ice storm hit and someone asked The Rancher about the roads, he might reply "slicker than snot on a shit-house door," reducing us boys to helpless hysteria. If that didn't do it, he'd hit us with "slicker than a preacher's dick in a calf's ass," and we would capitulate. Oh, we'd quote him, but we knew we could never outdo him or even approach the foothills of his genius.

Such pungent little phrases spiced up discourse among the farm folk, usually a little less spicy than The Rancher's. If The Parents had just bought something they might say "we hadn't worn the new off it yet." After being cooped up by a blizzard or rainstorm or illness there came a time to "go outside and blow the stink off." An especially shiftless person might get dubbed "worthless as tits on a boar," or if times grew tough, a farmer might threaten to "strap on a tin bill and pick shit with the chickens." The older farm folk might accuse a kid of just sitting around picking his nose and eating it, which usually triggered off an outburst of activity, however brief.

When pestered by someone or something, you might say the pesterer "made your heinie tired," heinie being a euphemism for buttocks. I told The Mother when she tried to put me to work one day that she made my heinie tired. She pared down my vocabulary immediately, and I deduced she didn't want to hear anything more about my heinie during my lifetime. I had no trouble going along with that.

ASIDE: To check the spelling of heinie I resorted to my online thesaurus, which offered the following: backside, behind, booty, bottom, breech, bum, buns, butt, caboose, can, cheeks, derriere, duff, fanny, fundament, hams, haunches, buttocks, hunkers, keister, nates, posterior, rear, rear end, rump, seat, tail, tail end, and tush. My spell checker whimpered for mercy.

The Father got a little more pungent when he said of a neighbor that he was so dumb he couldn't pour piss out of a boot with the directions written on the heel. After a drought he might refer to the weather as dryer than a popcorn fart. When the drought broke, as it always did, he might hope for a gully-washer, a trash-mover, or a toad-strangler; a heavy rain, in other words. When he really liked something, like a particular food, he might say "Boy, howdy" to express his pleasure. "Hunky-dory" was another expression of appreciation.

But all this country talk turned weak and insipid when compared to The Rancher:

"It's pretty hot, isn't it, Rancher?"

"Hotter than a virgin on the verge."

"Hotter than a fresh-fucked fox in a forest fire."

We couldn't compete.

The Father rarely used profanity, except under duress of the most trying. He would, to be sure, if a dog got too friendly or rambunctious, offer to kick a lung out of it, but he never did. He might also refer to some startled person as staring like a tromped-on toad. I heard one farmer after a pitch game say he had lost his ass and all its fixtures, a phrase I admired.

The Father employed a pair of draft horses, Brownie and Pet. These horses enjoyed both extreme strength and a symbiotic relationship with The Father; they pretty much understood one another. They didn't understand me, though. I'm not certain they ever realized I existed. At least when I tried to harness them they would ignore my best efforts and step on me instead. They had hooves the size of manhole covers, but the ground in the barn was soft. You might consider for a moment just why it was soft.

No one could ride these horses; many men tried, none succeeded. But I discovered I could ride around on them, albeit with not a hint of control. I recall bragging from Brownie's back while The Father milked a cow, pointing out my horse-riding superiority to all the men in the township. About then Brownie must have thought me a horsefly, because he twitched his hide and dumped me. I don't think I ever saw The Father laugh as hard as he did that time.

But times changed, and draft horses went out of style. I don't know if ours died or retired or what; I don't think The Father would have ever sold them. But he purchased a Case tractor, a pretty small machine, and used that for a while. He kept running into jobs too big for the Case, so he replaced it with a John Deere tractor of immense proportions and engine displacement. That proved satisfactory; he could hook it, like the draft horses, to anything he wanted to move—outbuildings, oil wells, court houses, whatever—and move it into a new location.

You get nothing for nothing; in retrospect Brownie and Pet seemed pleasant creatures; a tractor lacks charm. But eventually tractors replaced horses for our annual fall gathering to bring in the crops.

Harvest Time

Harvest time demanded the hardest work but also supplied us with social interaction. Neighboring farmers would combine their forces and go from farm to farm, harvesting and storing the grain.

First a farmer cut down the grain, then bound it into sheaves or bundles, then arranged the bundles into shocks; the individual farmer did all this in preparation for the threshing to separate grain from straw.

A dozen or so neighbors would bring wagons and horses and make relatively short work of the entire operation.

Farmers hired a local man who owned a tractor and a threshing machine to set up his equipment on each farm. The men gathered the grain and fetched it to the thresher, then pitched it into the machine's yawning maw.

The machine separated the straw and grain, so a farmer ended up with a large pile of straw and a wagonload of grain. They never took rest breaks but waiting in line to access the thresher gave the men a chance to cool off a bit. By noon men and beasts needed food and rest.

Typical shocks of grain, arranged to make them easier to collect and feed into the thresher. From the author's collection, but I don't remember where I got it.

The farmers' wives donated food and helped the landowner's wife prepare a monstrous meal: fried chicken, beef, coleslaw, mashed potatoes, corn, bread, cornbread, and a couple of hogsheads of iced tea and lemonade and cold milk. I tried to avoid the dishwashing afterward, only to get promoted to water boy.

So I carried water to the men as they worked; the Midwest can get a tad warm in the summer. A person didn't sweat much in that heat, though; perspiration evaporated almost immediately, what with the heat and the wind.

When I began my harvesting career I could look over the entire operation and see only one engine, the one on the tractor that powered the threshing machine. The crews used horses for everything else. By the time I retired and these harvesting practices changed during the last months of World War Two, the horses had all disappeared. The workers used pickups and tractors. We lost something, to be sure. Later farm equipment companies concocted a combine/harvester that pretty much did it all: harvested, threshed, and cleaned grain. They cost a whole batch of money, more than most farm families ever dreamed of accumulating. Everyone considered harvesting hot, dirty work; dust and straw permeated the entire operation.

One freethinking neighbor solved that problem and showed up for work wearing a hat, brogans, bib overalls, and not another stitch. He theorized that straw and chaff would fall all the way through his raiment and out of his life. In deference to the women he put on a shirt before coming to lunch lest he flash the cooks when he reached for the dumplings. The ladies still freaked out, but that's what they did best.

A threshing crew at work. The pile of straw is seen at the right, with the tractor on the left supplying power to the thresher. Courtesy Missouri Historical Society.

I didn't see it, but a harvest-time legend has it that while busy pitch-forking grain into the threshing machine's gullet a farmer suddenly let out a soul-searing scream. He then threw his pitchfork into the thresher (bringing the entire operation to a halt) and fell off his wagon. His comrades investigated and discovered a scorpion had stung the unfortunate on the head of his reproductive organ. They hauled the victim off to The Little Town Nearby and a physician, who treated him. After the crisis had passed, the victim's cohorts suggested that his remarkable swelling could have won quite a number of prizes, if they could just find the right contests. The victim ripped out some fairly brisk advice for them in return, approaching The Rancher's levels. I think modern medical practice has brought treatments for such problems up to date, but I don't care.

Baling Hay

A similar operation involved baling hay, usually alfalfa. Sometimes we baled prairie hay, a lush sort of tall grass, but not often. I never quite understood why, but I never asked about it, and no one ever volunteered any information.

In preparation a farmer would cut down the hay with a mowing machine, leveling about a five-foot swath. He then raked the hay into long rows in order to let it dry out; baling green alfalfa leads to spontaneous combustion, which burns down barns, which have to be rebuilt.

The driver steered the baler down the windrows; two men rode the rear of the machine, inserting wire (baling wire, a staple on a farm in those days) through the machine, then tying it off. As the hay progressed through the machine a large ram compressed it and thus created bales.

Windrows made the job easier for the baling machine, which followed the lines, ingesting the hay. It also ingested rocks and turtles and snakes that had burrowed into the windrows, creating no end of merry times for the men working further back on the baler. Blacksnakes merely diverted the men, but copperheads, being totally poisonous, made them jump off the baler and find impromptu weapons, such as pitchforks, large rocks, monkey wrenches, or the like.

An early, somewhat crude hay baler, this one pulled by a tractor. The sled is not attached, nor the seats for the men who inserted the wires to hold the bales together. From the author's collection.

The bales fell out of the back of the machine like so much Brontosaurus scat. Usually the men tied a “sled” to the back of the machine and found a middle-sized boy to work on it. Our sled consisted of five or six one by twelve boards with another board bolted across the front edge to hold it together.

During construction of this sled the creators left a gap between the middle boards. When the bales emerged, the middle-sized boy would stack them, four on the bottom level, three on the next, two after that, and one hernia-popping topper. After he hoisted the top one in place, and he had to be Johnny-at-the-rat-hole to manage this stunt, the boy picked up a five-foot steel bar with a pointed end and drove it into the ground between the middle boards. Theory held that the bar would stick in the ground, the sled would continue, and the pile of ten bales would slide off the sled neatly stacked for later pickup. Said middle-sized boy would then wrench the bar out of the ground and race back to catch the sled and repeat the procedure. This procedure, it was planned, left neat stacks of ten bales each around the field, facilitating picking them up later.

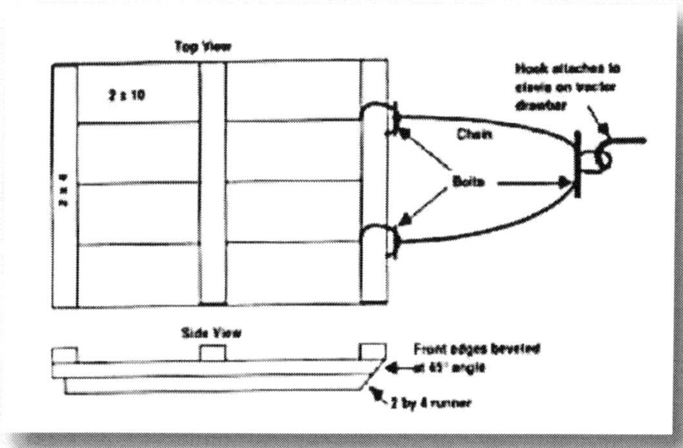

The general plan of a sled to drag behind a baling machine. The ones I knew were wooden, with a slot down the middle into which one could ram a steel pole, thereby sliding the bales off. No fun, especially, but it worked, usually. From the author's collection.

Well, that was the plan. It could go wrong in any number of ways. I've hunted around the farms in my county, looking for sleds, but turned up nothing; they're even using some small trailers now. The old wood sleds, unpainted, were left out to rot and disappear.

You might, instead of sticking the bar into the dirt, miss and jab the bar into your foot, causing you to speak directly to Jesus, Jove, and Allah. More commonly you might miss the crack and break one of the boards, causing a work stoppage and a general cussing out. Or the bar could come out of the ground before the bales all slid off, strewing the ten bales in a picturesque but random pattern. If you made that error, you could just bet the day of reckoning would come when you later collected the bales.

The best thing about working the sled? It made you incredibly, almost permanently, dirty; you worked in a dust cloud most of the time. You had to get naked and jump in a creek for preliminary cleaning before even approaching the house, otherwise the women would chase you away with brooms.

I recall stopping my car one day on a highway to gawk, open-mouthed, at large, cylindrical bales of hay, of which I had only heard rumors. What a chicken-doo-doo way to bale hay, I thought. On the other hand, the bales did not have to be put away because almost no haymows could hold them.

My favorite haymaking memory, though, involved the first two of The Sister's daughters, Creature One and Creature Two. They decided they would, during a visit, go to the fields with The Father (their grandfather) and help him make hay. They'd seen too many movies about farm life by then, one supposes, and so had begun to suffer from Disney Brain Rot.

So off we went, riding a rack wagon to the hay fields, Creatures One and Two giggling with anticipation. After about an hour of shoving hay around, Creature One asked The Father if it wasn't about time to start for home. The Father explained they really "hadn't got started good yet."

This depressed Creatures One and Two, but they soldiered on. I laughed inwardly, hollowly and harshly; I realized by then that life was only ashes, and they would find no joy in the hay field. After lunch Creature One claimed to have developed a headache and so must refrain from further haying. Instead she'd take the afternoon off to read, a sure cure for a headache. Creature Two decided to stay home and tend to her. The haying went faster without their help. One taste of putting up hay was enough for the Creatures; they never offered to help again.

Storing Hay

We didn't just leave the hay in the field lest it rot. Barns had second stories called haymows, and while kids found them a wonderful place to fool around, the architects intended them to hold hay, baled or loose.

An illustration of men bringing loose hay to the haymow for storing, before the days of labor-saving devices like bales or slings or anything like that. Notice the bend in the ground man's pitchfork; it's bent because he is hefting a gigantic fork full of hay up to his partner.

You might well imagine this sort of damned foolishness drove me off the farm and into the wide world of anything else, to work indoors, preferably sitting down. Courtesy of The State Historical Society of Missouri.

A sling full of baled hay being lifted into the haymow. When the sling reached the peak of the barn roof, the load of bales went on into the barn. Courtesy Missouri Historical Society.

In the early days men would pitch the hay onto the rack wagons, take it to the barn, and then pitch the hay into the haymow. This procedure brought about aching backs and aching everything else, so some genius somewhere devised a set of three slings and a rope and pulley arrangement to take the hay into the mow with a minimum of effort, sweat, and cursing. For loose hay we used three slings and a rack wagon, a sling being a sort of hammock device consisting of two halves with a catch in the middle and a trip rope. Men piled hay on one sling until they considered it full, then they placed another sling load on top of the first load. When they had the second sling full, they put the last one on and filled it, then headed for the barn.

Upon arrival the driver took the horses (or tractor) to the rear of the barn and hitched them to a rope that ran through pulleys and up to the haymow at the highest point of the roof and out over the wagon full of hay. A hook on a pulley would be lowered to the wagon; the two ends of the top sling attached thereto, and the signal given to the man with the horses or tractor. He would pull away from the barn, and the rope would tighten, lifting the sling full of hay up from the wagon and into an open door on the barn's second story. If all went well, the sling would engage a track in the top of the barn and could then be positioned inside as desired.

When the sling full of hay seemed appropriately placed, a man in the haymow would yank the trip rope; the two halves of the sling separated, and a third of a wagon load of hay dropped into the haymow. Men with pitchforks later moved the hay to the sides of the mow or wherever the owner preferred.

Once more flaws developed. Sometimes the guy in the haymow would pull the trip rope prematurely and drop the hay on himself. Usually he could crawl out again while his friends and neighbors rolled around having laughing fits. Then, too, the sling might come apart as it lifted off the wagon, leaving you the next sling with two-thirds of a wagonload of hay in it, causing stress in the whole mechanism if you tried to lift it. This made the men pretty goosey when they tried to double up the load, but they often succeeded. But if the second sling went bad you didn't try to lift a triple load of hay; you just got your pitchforks and started heaving the hay into the mow by brute force, cursing an evil providence and promising to repent for any number of sins, real or imaginary.

Baled hay caused different problems. A normal-sized bale in those days was about eighteen inches square and three or four feet long, weighing fifty to seventy pounds. Chunky little rascals. So we would put the bales on a wagon; one man drove, two more hoisted the bales onto the wagon, and a fourth guy arranged the bales. At this time the expertise of the sled boy came to their attention; they preferred to have the bales neatly stacked, not strewn all over hell and gone.

I learned from this that whatever actions I might take, sure enough there would be a day of reckoning. I found this insight valuable for the rest of my days and still do. I don't always like it, of course, but I've learned to live with it, more or less.

I recall once The Father drove the tractor while some other guy and I threw the bales onto the wagon. The pace picked up if a rainstorm headed our way (in the Midwest you can see a storm coming a couple of area codes away) or if we spotted a small tornado cavorting about on the horizon. The Father decided not to waste any time; I think he just wired the tractor throttle down as we raced from stack to stack, hurling bales onto the wagon. Of course, the more bales you get on the wagon, the higher you have to heave the next ones. There's a moral in this, perhaps even a life pattern, if philosophy could only discover it. But we usually outran the rain and wind by a comfortable margin, then puked for a while.

Sometimes we could just stack the bales out in the open; the farmer depended on the bales' density to keep them from rotting when the rains came. That usually worked. But other times nothing would do except putting the bales into the barn by one of two methods. The first was to heave them into a second-story window in the barn where they would be taken over by another worker and deployed as desired. Once again, stacking those heavy little mothers would draw all the poisons in your system out to your skin, where they would drop off as sweat and eat little holes in the haymow floor.

ASIDE: OK, that didn't really happen, I just made it up. But it sure as hell felt that way.

The second method arrived just after World War Two; a device with a track in it, powered by a tractor, onto which you could dump the bales and happily watch them disappear into the haymow. We rejoiced at this technology, but the men in the haymow still had to stack them higher and higher.

The bale lifter viewed from the side. A tractor supplied power to the track which carried the bales into the haymow. I have no idea where The Father obtained this device or what it cost. But I didn't care then, and I don't care now. Photo by the author.

The corrugated iron roof over the haymow transmitted heat most efficiently. During an August hot spell the haymow underneath said roof would grow something more than warm. That heat discouraged throwing sixty-pound bales five and six high to stash them away, but the job demanded exactly that. A zephyr, breezy but way short of cool, might pass through the haymow now and again, proving the power of prayers and curses.

And the dust choked off one's breath and left him spitting out mudballs for days afterward. Bale heavers began to dream of other means of existence, or at least this one did. I began to dream of less dirt and fewer heavy things to lift. I'd have to take up some other line of work to attain that, I began to realize.

Balls

Quite a lot of farm work happened in or around the barn. The Father built a sort of birthing room out of straw bales for his ewes when he raised sheep for a few years. Otherwise the little mothers would go to the farthest corner of the farm during a blizzard to drop a lamb, and we would have to go fetch the mother and child, lest the youngster freeze into a lamb-sickle. Since delivery could develop complications The Father devised various crude but effective methods of assisting the procedure, such as a set of wire-stretchers, a multiple block and tackle arrangement.

When a male beast grew to sufficient size, the animal husbandry philosophies of the time demanded castration so the critter would grow fatter and more docile. Bull calves became steers, whether they liked it or not; boar hogs got The Treatment; rams became placid after being tended to.

Lucky me, I got to help.

In our area some farmers performed these operations using only a very sharp pocketknife. Indeed, according to legend, one of our neighbors castrated pigs by biting the scrotum cords in two, but no one ever proved this to my satisfaction. I don't recall anyone ever joshing him about it, either. I'd like to have had the film rights, if he actually did it that way.

The Father sent off for a device, a castrating clamp, built on the general plan of a bolt-cutter. The Sears catalog had other items for sale: Castrating Knives, Teat Dilators, Horse Tooth Floats, Horse Balling Guns, and Horse Mouth Speculums. Except for the knife, I have no idea what these other things were for. I speculated about some of them, but I never worked up the courage to ask The Father, and I sure as thunder wasn't going to ask The Mother.

ADVICE: As I recall, one of the early Mondo movies from the 1960s featured such a stunt. When my wife asked how I liked the movie, I explained that a pretty blonde Nordic type girl had been filmed gnawing the gonads off a reindeer. I was impressed; Gene Autry never tried anything like that. Tarzan may have, but I didn't see that movie. I sure would have, had it played in my area. It would have been a unbeatable Saturday afternoon matinee.

While we were castrating calves once The Father looked at me during a respite and mused aloud, "You know, I could save you a lot of trouble." My testicles shot up to just beneath my tonsils, but he dropped the subject.

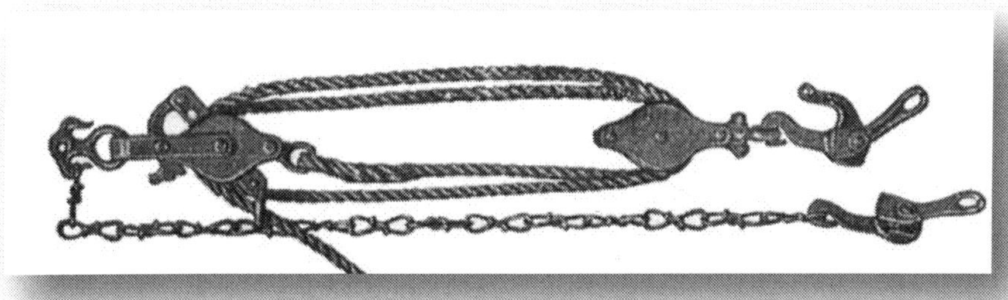

A pair of wire-stretchers, designed to tighten up wire fences. This device would, however, also withdraw recalcitrant baby animals from their mommas. Photo from an old catalog I found lying around; I have not the slightest idea where it came from..

Your average beast of the field does not care to have his maleness removed by gnawing, knifing, or clamping, so someone had to incapacitate the critter. For large creatures a sort of collapsible stall immobilized the brute while the operation proceeded. The men would just gorilla down smaller animals by brute strength and hold them to meet their fate. A yearling calf, I found, could have done fairly well in the World Wrestling Federation.

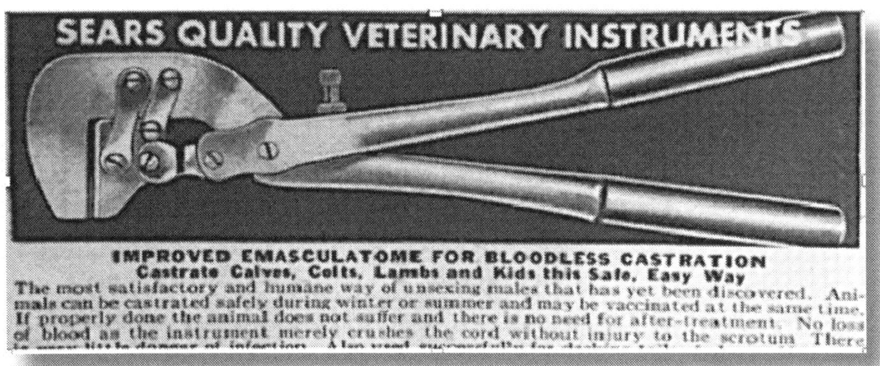

A clamp used for castration. On the second line under the picture you can read this clamp works to "castrate calves, colts, lambs and kids." I'm reasonably sure that "kids" here meant baby goats. From the author's collection.

Castrating did not represent the worst of barnyard medicine, though. Occasionally calves developed screwworms, an infection in the navel, which resulted in a mass of maggots. Nothing would do for it but to catch the calf, hog-tie it, scrape out the mass of white wiggly wormlets, and pour in a dollop of carbolic acid. This usually did the trick, but that calf would jump a four-strand barbed wire fence for a year or so if you got close to him again.

Lo, the Former Manure Spreader

The barn required yet another task I grew to loathe: cleaning it out. Farms contain lots of animals, and we kept busy feeding those animals. Although the animals were commodities, they also were all-conference defecators. Someone had to deal with all that defecation, in itself a commodity of sorts. Although unpleasant to deal with, it was not to be ignored or left to return to the soil; the fecal matter had value as fertilizer. I didn't like to think about that, but there it was, a fact of life.

The manure served as fertilizer for our vegetable garden, for example, and it seemed to work. Working on larger tracts, such as an alfalfa field, necessitated spreading it over the entire patch. That meant someone had to load it into some sort of transportation device, take it to the site, and spread it around. This constituted superb training for a career in higher education, but I didn't know that at the time.

The Father owned a device for spreading manure; the manufacturer, nothing if not pragmatic, called it a manure spreader. This was a low, smallish wagon with a sort of slow treadmill for a floor. This floor would creep towards the rear of the wagon, where rotating tines would scatter the manure, like politicians. The driver stayed up front using either horses or a tractor to propel the device.

Just as the advertisement says, a manure spreader, back in the days when they used horses to pull them. By the time I got the job we had a tractor, which made it easier. I believe The Father bought his manure spreader from Sears for $120, but that didn't include the horses. Or the manure. From the author's collection.

As you know, barnyard manure tends to clump, and unless it had had a chance to dry out, did not generate much dust. When The Mother and I cleaned out the chicken house, however, what we got into the manure spreader was very dry indeed, dusty, crumbly, easily broken up. The rotating tines would pulverize this manure, but if I kept moving into the wind I might survive.

The Midwest doesn't lack for winds, but they generally blew only one direction at a time, except for tornados. Keeping my nose to the wind would imply spreading manure in a straight line for a few miles, which wouldn't do; The Father wanted all our manure to go onto our own fields. So I had to turn around at the end of a pass and come back with the wind. If the breeze blew just right, that meant I could make that pass while surrounded on all sides by a cloud of powdered manure, me, the manure spreader, and the horses, all going along at the same rate. Passers-by might break into "I Love a Parade."

Eventually I had to inhale. Years later I saw my first air filter mask in a hardware store and wondered if they had existed in the old days. This kind of work further stimulated my fantasies about making an escape from that farm, or any other farm, for that matter, indeed, the very concept of farms I began to find rather off-putting.

In point of fact, a lever on the manure spreader engaged and disengaged the moving floor, so one could stop the floor and go back to the beginning and make another pass into the wind. Strangely enough, no one ever explained that lever to me. If they had, I suspect it would have taken me twice as long to deliver the fertilizer to the fields. I'm sure of it, in fact.

All that dealing with doo-doo did nothing to endear me to farm life. I vigorously sought information about other professions than farming, and I discovered they were there to be had. My brother became a chemist, and my brother-in-law took up carpet and tile laying. I found chemistry great fun, but carpet laying had no discernable appeal for me, In due time I lost interest in chemistry, as well, and turned to other means making a living. I dreamed of an inside job, preferably with air conditioning Preferably with me sitting in a nice easy chair.

I really didn't hate farm life, the food was good and we had plenty of it, but I continued to fantasize about leaving the farm. And leave it I did. Little did I realize that except for a couple of years spent in a factory I would spend the rest of my life in schools of varying sizes, like the one in the next chapter.

CHAPTER SIX

HIGH SCHOOL, OR, O, BRAVE NEW WORLD! (not)

So I left The One-Room Country Grade School and enrolled in The High School in The Little Town Nearby. Both my siblings had attended the same high school and survived, with honors even, and now my turn came around. Agog at the prospect, I savored the thought of attending school with hundreds of students rather than a dozen or so and spending a lot more time in The Little Town Nearby. The High School was situated just on the south side of the downtown area, such as it was. But that area contained the drug store hangout for teens, where many of us gathered after the last class. The juke box had the latest hits on it; you put in a nickel and you could shuffle around for three minutes of music, anything from Spike Jones to "Saber Dance." No, we didn't try to dance to those, but we had some Glenn Miller available, too. Pretty syrupy, but slow dancing taught us the difference between hot girls and the other kind.

But first I had to get from The Little House on the Prairie, Part Three, to The High School.

Wagon Loads of Advice

People lined up as far as the state line to give me free advice. The Brother, whose recommendations I held in most esteem, suggested that I sign up for Algebra and Latin I. The Bad Little Girl from The Country Grade School, aghast at the thought, exclaimed, "But those things are hard!" All along I suspected country folks didn't aspire to higher degrees of learning; their style just didn't include that. I'd hear them say things like "That's not for the likes of us!" I later deduced that this country copout absolved them from considerable responsibility. They seemed to take some pride in their humility. They didn't seem to aspire to more than they already had, but then what's a heaven for?

All the more reason for me to find new horizons, separating myself further from my rusticity. Long ago, back in Chapter One, I knew I wanted something other than farm life. Most of the country boys signed up for Agriculture courses when they entered high school, and when I didn't the Agriculture teacher came out to speak to The Father and rat me out. The Father told him he didn't need the teacher's help raising me and to leave his boy alone. I suspect he knew The Brother advised me about high school, but in any event, I call down blessings on both of them; they did me right. At age thirteen I began a college preparatory sequence of courses albeit totally innocent and ignorant of what people did in college. I'd find out later. Would I ever.

Getting There, Again

But first I had to somehow get myself into The Little Town Nearby. I couldn't ride my horse five miles to The High School; for one thing the school lacked facilities for horses. Besides, I didn't have a horse any more. Laws prohibited my driving a car at that tender age, and I'd never owned a bicycle; those gravel roads would shred bicycle tires in about a half mile.

So someone had to haul me in, and someone had to tote me back. Because The Brother worked in town he toted me both ways. Luckily, I had some time to kill after school before I met him to ride home. Usually that meant strolling over to The Carnegie Public Library, descending into the basement where the kiddy books awaited, and figuring out ways to sneak up to the upper levels for the grownup stuff.

> *ASIDE: By the way, Dale Carnegie (1835-1919) amassed about 4.8 billion bucks in modern equivalency and began funding libraries around the nation. Our library cost $15,000 in 1902. Carnegie is buried in the Sleepy Hollow Cemetery, North Tarrytown, New York, and if you get there before I do, please put a rose on his grave. He brightened up my salad days immensely and I will be grateful to him as long as I have consciousness.*

The Brother hauling me back and forth worked for a year or so.

A 1929 Pontiac coupe, very similar to mine. I don't remember what became of it, but when The Father obtained a 1948 Dodge, I took over his 1938 Dodge. We played automotive move-up, as it were. From the author's collection of fond memories.

When I came of age (16) I bought a car, a 1929 Pontiac. Cost me $100. My Aunt sold it to me. Looked a lot like a Model T Ford. That rather changed things. For the better, I thought, but the jury was out on that judgement for about a year. The Parents gave me strict instructions never to drive it downtown, only from home to The High School, and of course I wouldn't dream of doing such a thing.

That Pontiac solved my transportation problems and set me free. The spokes in the wheels were wooden, as were the running boards, but you could substitute a pine 1" x 12" for the latter. I found out soon enough that if I hit a bump too hard both doors would unlatch and fly open, which was worrisome. The front bumper was a four-inch steel pipe, basic, but functional. That car served me well for a few years, and I loved it. I loved it more than any car I ever owned, till in the 1980s I invested in a Triumph TR6. That comes later.

The Building

The building for The High School presented new amazements. It didn't have just one floor and one room; it had four floors with more rooms and closets and halls than I could count. I found boys' facilities on every floor, but with my newly gained familiarity with flush toilets, I coped. Each class was assigned a different room, so this old country boy had to blaze a trail to five different rooms for five different teachers and five different subjects.

About this time the farm kids and I split the blanket. They went to the basement and began butchering hogs; I went to Latin and Algebra and did the best I could. I considered most of them decent guys, but I never regretted that separation. For that matter, neither did they, as I recall. We parted on friendly terms, but we just didn't have much in common any more. I had cast myself adrift, for sure.

Classes and Teachers

My transcript records that I took four classes plus Physical Education that first year. The High School also had a rather silly practice called Home Room. For that I went to a classroom and heard the news for the day, not about politics or hunting or anything of substance, but the school functions for the day. Convocations, class elections, like that. This gave me a chance to catch up on my homework, ogle the girls, and swap the latest dirty jokes.

"Hey, did you hear about the plastic surgeon who hung himself?"

My school day began with English 9, or Ninth Grade (freshman) English, and I don't remember a damned thing about it. I had a teacher, the old maid who worked the evening shift in the Public Library. Do I recall a single thing I read? Not a bit of it. I may have diagrammed sentences, a practice that's fallen out of favor, sad to say. Nevertheless, it remains the most valuable activity I experienced in an English class, until we read some Shakespeare. We'd done some diagramming in grade school. I think I could still do it, if paid enough.

Next came Latin I. "*Amo, amas, amat*," and like that. Taught by another aging harridan, this one with red hair in tight curls from The Flaming Twenties. But we had reached the Flaccid Forties; she must have kept the hairdo from her youth. I got by. Studying sentence structure in Latin taught me more about English grammar than I learned in English classes, even when we diagrammed.

All this pretty much stupefied me, but then I next went to General Science, in which I kicked ass and took numbers. When The Brother had taken college Chemistry and Physics I'd looked over his shoulder while he did his homework. He had, you recall, bought me a chemistry set with all manner of smelly experiments to do, and I did them all several times and made up some of my own. And I read his textbooks over weekends. So when the General Science teacher cum football coach asked if any of us could distinguish between a physical change and a chemical change, I spoke right up and submitted that "A chemical change alters the molecular structure; a physical change does not." Silence fell like a thunderclap. Most of the jocks slowly swiveled around to stare, and three ugly girls fell in love with me. I began to make my bones that day.

My emerging from the pack made the city kids aware of me. I'd known a few of them from church, but the gulf between city kids and farm kids remained several parsecs wide. The townies had enjoyed one another's company since the first grade, so they didn't need farm kids, especially.

During a lunch break everyone took brown bags to a cafeteria on the fourth floor. My acceptance became a certainty when some of the city kids began to invite me to sit with them. It seemed a long way off the farm, and I liked it a lot.

A Basic Algebra course followed lunch. I recall the teacher as another old maid, slightly attractive, and she may have had a wooden leg. I did all right in there; algebra was a game of balancing, just like inorganic chemistry. No problem, and I began to goof off and spend more time helping other students than taking care of my own grades.

But that paid off in a sort of a way. The School Board in their Olympian wisdom decreed that all students must take physical education. Running around in our underwear would be good for us, they thought.

Boys and girls repaired to their appropriate gymnasiums, widely separated, and put on our little shorts and played various games. Weather permitting, we played a sort of football.

Although we had played rudimentary touch football in The Country Grade School, what we did in gym class reflected the actual game more closely. Every so often I got handed the ball, then turned up field and ran like a proverbial deer, often scoring a touchdown.

I had never dreamed I had this talent, nor did any sane person. But then came that awful day when two guys from Algebra I'd tutored didn't come to class, and I got creamed at the line of scrimmage. Those two guys, both starting backs on the varsity team, had been running cover for me every time we played football. I thereafter shied away from the football like a nervous pony at a culvert.

And that ended the day. We showered, dressed, and went about our teenybopper pursuits. Those might involve the Public Library, the drug store, or later a pool room.

Many, many years later I came to find out I hadn't needed to attend gym class. The school had a rule that if any student went to the library and wrote a one-page essay, he or she would be excused from gym. Did they ever tell me about that? Hell, no.

And I loved our little library. But then I never met a library I didn't love, from the little room in the Country Grade School to the Library of Congress or the British Library. I began to realize that Heaven had nothing to do with harps and halos, it was more likely some kind of library.

At least I hoped so.

Extracurricular Stuff

I began to notice that many of the students after school participated in more or less organized activities. Cheerleaders practiced leading cheers, for instance, and I had hot eyes for one of the cheerleaders, a short Jane Wyman looking sort of a girl, but I was wasting my time. While she wasn't the only pebble on the beach, I thought she was the roundest. The only time I asked her for a date she said her grandmother had just died. Six decades later, I still don't believe it. A classmate later told me she moved to Miami Beach and became a hooker. Serves her right.

But I digress.

I made new friends. One good buddy and I shared many adventures, like peeking into the girly show at the county fair by cutting a small hole in the back of the tent. We couldn't sec the stage, but we could gawk into the dressing rooms. That was enough, almost too much.

Every July Fourth he and I and some other rinky-dinks would repair to a city park with aerial bombs, single shots and repeaters. Taking shelter behind trees and one another we fired these bombs horizontally as gunfighs and had a wonderful time.

One Fourth my buddy didn't show up for the Park War, so we went by his house to fetch him. We decided, though, not to knock on the door but to bombard his front porch till he came out to join us.

Who would have guessed his father, a railroad foreman, had boozed himself bulletproof the night before and was sleeping on that front porch? He awoke to a half dozen or more aerial bombs going off around him. Not a good way to wake up cold sober; with a hangover it must have been a foretaste of Hell. We could have stayed and apologized, but we didn't.

One afternoon my buddy and I watched our school baseball team play. The game didn't look all that difficult to me, although they used a smaller, harder ball than I was used to from playing "move up" in The Country Grade School.

That day watching our high school team, luckily for me, a player tried to stretch a single into a double and slid into second base, cleats high. Hard. Our second baseman waited for him and tagged him out, but it cost him about a four-inch gash in his leg. They took him to a local physician for flushing out and sewing up. My interest in playing baseball bottomed out that day. Too butch.

But a few days later my buddy suggested we drop by play tryouts. The Junior High School staged a production every spring, an annual fiasco. The director/English teacher had chosen a dramatic thunderbolt entitled *Hooray for Youth!,* the kind of script for which no one charged royalties, probably out of shame. This particular drama made *Aaron Slick from Punkin Creek* look like *Hamlet, Prince of Denmark.*

But my friend and I went to auditions. The director conducted the tryouts; we all read aloud from the script. That cheerleader with the bangs tried out, bless her heart, and so did my buddy.

When the cast list went up did the cheerleader or my pal get cast? Not a bit. But did I? You bet your bird. Since the rehearsals took place after classes in the afternoon, getting to them was no problem, and so I fell into the mock heroics of educational theatre. Not very educational, and barely qualifying as theatre, but away I went.

I wonder sometimes about roads not taken, but it's too late.

Years later when I saw the movie *Porky's* I thought it an astonishingly accurate depiction of high school life; it certainly resembled my high school experience. The movie had a character that appeared in all the school plays; I played this role nicely in my own high school. For many years I had a script folded once and tucked into my right hip pocket. I thus entered a world of pretending to be what I wasn't, and I was to stay with it for a considerable time. I received substantial support for this. At first.

And so my first year blundered to a close. I don't recall what I did that summer; I probably read some more. Nothing assigned or silly like that, but stuff I picked up in the grownups' section of the public library.

By then I had devised a system for accessing the sex education books in the library. Librarians in those days put such books on shelves directly in front of their checkout desk, to keep an eye on which dirty little boys or dirty old men might be looking them over.

But I beat the system. By studying the distribution of the sex books I decided to go for the fourth one from the right on the top shelf. A small book bursting with drawings of various odds and ends.

I sauntered over to that shelf with a few other books in my hands; set them on top of the shelves and pretended to examine them, while feeling along the shelved books till I came to the one I wanted. I slid it out while the librarian was busy and added it to my other books. I then retired to one of the reading rooms, quite out of sight from the suspicious librarians.

Well, it wasn't a Sears catalog, that's for sure. Neither was it *Playboy* or *Penthouse*, but it was the best we could do. Various drawings of human plumbing answered a few questions. True, some graphics resembled maps of the Malay Peninsula, but it was a start. By repeating this scheme with other books I gained a bit more information. I never returned those books to their shelves, though; I just added them somewhere else, like with the Tarzan books. The librarians didn't know where they were, but I did. Eventually I'd put them out somewhere so the librarians could find and re-shelve them. I couldn't be bothered; I was too busy gathering data and mulling it over. It was ever thus.

What a shame that library didn't subscribe to *The National Geographic.* But now I have the complete set on DVDs. I still wonder why they thought it was all right to print brown boobs, but not white ones. Or pink, for that matter.

But a curious young kid would have to get to the new copies of *National Geographic* first, before other horny young scholars carved the pages into tattered ruins. I've seen it happen in far larger libraries.

The Sophomore Year

I anticipated with great glee my move from The Lower Depths of Junior High School to the sophisticated high life of Senior High School. I didn't know what that meant, but I suspected good things lay ahead. And indeed they did.

The *Oxford English Dictionary*, than which there exists no more definitive source for word meanings, defines sophomore as:

> *. . . characteristic of a sophomore; hence, pretentious, bombastic, inflated in style or manner; immature, crude, superficial.*

That pretty much nails it, a sense of superiority based on nothing whatsoever. We sneered at ninth graders because we were tenth graders.

The courses grew tougher, even if the students didn't. My day began with English 10, taught by a pretty foxy babe who had just joined the faculty. She assigned *Julius Caesar*, Shakespeare's shortest and least sexy play, to read aloud. Even so we all chortled at lines like "we are undone!" I managed to miss the point of *Julius Caesar* altogether; I thought it ended when they slipped the shiv to Big Julie.

That year Laurence Olivier's film of *Hamlet* came to our little town, and the English teacher arranged to have all her classes see it. I asked if I could sit by her; she purred a bit and agreed to that. I think I disappointed her when I said I wanted to be able to ask her about the parts I didn't understand. She's since died, passed on, but I still have some questions.

Biology came next, a traditionally sophomoric course in which entire armies of frogs died for our education. I didn't like the teacher, and the teacher didn't like me; I had grown a touch cocky by then. My lab partner in frog maiming got a better grade than I did because I helped her.

Then Geometry. I got along OK; theorems seemed interesting. Had the teacher included a little history of how geometry originated it would have worked better, I think. How, for instance, did the Greeks come so close to deducing the diameter of the earth? How did the Athenians build the Parthenon with just hand tools and a mob of slaves? I would have appreciated *entasis*, given the chance. The information stunned me when I learned that the Parthenon has hardly any straight lines in it; the architects used optical illusions in their designs and curved things.

The pillars on the short ends of the Parthenon, for example, are tipped slightly towards one another. If extended, they would meet a mile and a half over the Acropolis. Wow.

When I actually got to the Acropolis, I hunkered down by the short end of the Parthenon and peered along the side. Sure enough, there's a bulge in the floor. Makes it look better, they tell me. I remain very curious as to how they discovered that optical illusion, to say nothing of how they went about achieving it. I've heard a trench along the temple's side filled with water gave them a base horizontal, and they went from there.

Geometry ended, and I made another trip to the cafeteria, with music and dancing (I didn't dance. I still don't. I never will.) We could look out the windows and down upon the agriculture students as they lugged tubs of hog guts out of the basement. I gave thanks.

I had no clue then, but the next two classes, the two after lunch when sleep was most likely to come over most sophomores, became in retrospect the most valuable ones I took. First came Latin II, which described Caesar, coming, seeing, and whupping up on the natives. Young men have a taste for fascism, I understand, and this worked for me. I might well have taken Latin III and met Cicero, but it didn't happen because my college prep course only required two years of foreign language. Besides, no one taught Latin III.

The Romans being the bad guys in church and the good guys in Latin I and II didn't help my state of confusion. I began to suspect they were pretty good guys, but with a few faults, like the rest of us. A valuable lesson, that, that has continued to make a lot of sense.

A younger teacher offered the second course, Typing, as a high point finish for the day. She drilled and tested all of us pretty near to death, which seemed the only way one could learn to type, and I'm using a QWERTY keyboard to enter this into my iMac. She committed matrimony over some vacation or other, probably Christmas, so my buddies and I speculated about her sex life just as if we knew anything about such things. We were getting a little more sophisticated, but not from experience, only from speculations and fantasizing. We needed help but didn't get it and really didn't know where to go to ask. The next year we did.

I auditioned for another play, this one a legitimate script requiring royalties. I meandered onstage for a few scenes as a kind of 1920s Joe College, raccoon coat and all. My first line should have been, “Oh, there’s no need to do that,” but my synapses took a holiday, and I squeaked out, “Oh, there’s no nude to dee that,” then whipped around to see why the audience had exploded. I survived, but worse lay ahead.

The Pool Hall Downtown

Late in my sophomore year I discovered The Pool Hall Downtown, a favorite pleasure spa for lots of high school boys and a haunt of The Brother. A certain percentage of our classmates grooved on the guidance in Sunday School and would not darken the door of such a place. Another percentage hung out in other even worse sinks of vice and depravity if they could find one, which they could, just east of town. A friend and I went in once, but we didn’t feel welcome and so departed.

Teens couldn’t buy beer in The Pool Hall Downtown; the owner saw to that, but we could certainly play various types of table games. Those games included pocket billiards, a.k.a. pool, in various manifestations, the more difficult game of snooker, and even billiards on a table with no pockets. Three rail billiards is the most difficult of all the games, but some of the local citizens became rather skillful at it, including The Brother. Indeed, I watched him play in the finals of a city tournament, sponsored by The Pool Hall Downtown. I don't actually recall who won, The Brother or the other guy. I wish I did.

ASIDE: A lot of guys preferred eight ball or straight pool or even rotation, a child's game. You could play any game for money, but gamblers usually chose pea pool or nine ball. Snooker led in popularity, and I had a sucker on the ropes one day when I looked up into the eyes of The Father, who had dropped in for a beer. I calmly re-chalked my cue and shot the seven ball into the cue ball, which is not the way the Big Boys played the game.

A typical pool hall of the 1950s, although not the one in which I was raised; it doesn't exist anymore. Most pool halls had fewer tables than this one; I recall the one I frequented had two pool tables, four snooker tables, and one billiard table. From the author's collection.

Females rarely appeared in The Pool Hall Downtown, although an escort might treat them to a beer up front. A unisex toilet facility may have had something to do with it, as did societal pressures. Our high school girl friends itched to see what attracted us to the place, but they couldn't be lured in to find out.

The Pool Hall Downtown gave me an opportunity to try my first cigarette, picking up an opponent's smoke as we played pool. It didn't seem too bad, but it led to daily smoking, casualness, needless expense, and stinking clothes. As I was driving my 1929 Pontiac along a country road, I inhaled a non-filtered Camel cigarette for the first time. My body tried to tell me something that day, but I didn't wreck the car, so I smoked for the next fifty years. Let those without sin cast the first stone.

So in college I smoked cigarettes. In graduate school I switched to a pipe. That was cheaper. Toward the end of my teaching career I switched to bladder cancer and re-thought the entire matter.

The Rack Boy

The Rack Boy, who presided over the gaming area, had a lot to do. He re-racked the balls after every game and collected the fees. Another duty included cleaning out spittoons, wearing a very thick pair of gloves, gloves grown old and brown in the service.

When the draft beer supply ran out up front, he went to the basement to fetch up a keg through a good-sized trap door between the snooker tables. Of course, he had to leave that door open while he went below, and occasionally some idiot, usually tanked up on beer, would step backwards into it. High school guys would applaud and cry out, "Encore! Encore! Do it again." But you can't hurt a drunk. Kill them, yes, but you can't just hurt one.

The Rack Boy had many talents. He possessed a definitive collection of 78-rpm jazz recordings, and that's how I discovered jazz. High school kids liked it, and when our elders expressed utter disgust with it, that enhanced its charms all the more. The Mother used to say that the man who invented swing ought to.

The Rack Boy seemed to be enjoying The Good Life, even on his measly salary. If you wanted to hear "Dinner Music for A Pack of Hungry Cannibals," he had it. The same with "Celery Stalks at Midnight."

ASIDE: I could make up stuff like this, but I'm not, this time. "Dinner Music," a composition by the certifiably mad Raymond Scott, can be heard in some Roadrunner cartoons. "Celery Stalks" became such a standard that Lawrence Welk's gang of goody-goods played it. Even Doris Day recorded it. You can look it up.

Or for that matter, the ever-popular "It Must Be Jelly 'Cause Jam Don't Shake Like That!"

We might hear a few bars of jazz on the radio, but otherwise we had to go to The Music Store. In those days if you wanted to hear a recording at that store, you entered a small closet containing a record player, played the record for yourself, over and over, until you memorized it and decided you didn't need to buy it. I didn't have access to a record player, anyway.

But The Rack Boy's cleverness extended to other fields; he possessed and shared (may his tribe increase) more pornography than any of us knew existed. Some of us might have obtained a few photos from older brothers or a local pervert, but once again, The Rack Boy seemed to have it all.

His collection grew in importance, especially for the city guys who hadn't grown up on farms. Parents seemed dedicated to keeping their kids as ignorant as possible about sex for as long as possible, motivated by I know not what. Fear of some sort, I suppose. But their viewpoint resulted in amazing stupidity on the part of young, horny males. One such rustic admitted he had used a piece of string, "tied real tight," as a birth control device. Another sprinkled milk on his turgid manhood, then offered it to a calf; he almost became the county's first eunuch. Amusing, sort of, but this ignorance wrecked lives, fostered by adults who could have helped but didn't. I couldn't understand it then, and I can't understand it now. But I guess our elders thought sex education should come to us in pool halls, back seats, and locker rooms, but not, God forbid, in a classroom taught by an informed sex educator. Go figure.

Playboy and *Penthouse* appeared later to enlighten us with their airbrushed depictions of womankind. I was idly thumbing through the stroke magazines in the pool hall one day when a delivery man brought in a stack of the first issue of *Playboy*. A dozen copies as I recall; what they would be worth today I'd rather not think about. But I picked up a copy and read most of it. It didn't really make me want to rape and pillage and kill, but it was entertaining. I read the next six hundred issues of *Playboy*, though, twelve a year for fifty years. You can do the math.

But we had The Rack Boy's porn to tide us over. Love is not only where you find it but also how you manifest it. We figured all that out in The Pool Hall Downtown; Sunday school kind of glossed over it.

Under these conditions his dirty pictures offered considerable information about The Deed and how it was done.

“My God, can you do that?”

“Doesn’t that hurt?”

“You can’t knock her up doing that, can you?”

And we all profited from the Rack Boy’s advice on social interaction:

"When in doubt, whip it out."

“With a gentleman, it’s always tits first.”

This is the last page or dénouement *of one of the classic eight-pagers, "Sand Up Your Ass." From the author’s classic collection.*

The Rack Boy’s porn collection enhanced his income; he would occasionally sell some of his stuff. Eight-pagers cost five bucks, a tidy sum. Great fun, those little goodies. Eight-pagers were small pornographic pamphlets, usually containing eight poorly drawn pages about four by three inches, with a heavier cover stock. They first appeared in the late 1920s and finally petered out after World War Two. A comprehensive history, illustrated, may be found in *Tijuana Bibles: Art and Wit in America's Forbidden Funnies, 1930s-1950s*, by Bob Adelman, published in 1997 by Simon & Schuster. I recommend it. It's out of print now, but quite a lot of material turns up on the Internet if you type "Tijuana Bibles" into your browser. You can find them on eBay, too, at inflated prices. Depends on what you think they're worth, I guess.

Many featured celebrities or comic strip heroes. Betty Boop, Li'l Abner, Popeye, Mae West, Lassie (!), Amos and Andy, Clark Gable, Mickey Mouse, Cary Grant, Gert Babbo (Greta Garbo), Donald Duck, and Snow White and the Seven Dwarfs. We never looked at the funny papers quite the same way again. Blondie had talents we never imagined, as did Alley Oop and Rin Tin Tin.

Rumors had it that 8mm. black and white stag films existed and could be purchased. Sweaty perverts showed them at VFW stags, but high school guys couldn't get into those. Now anyone can call them up on a computer. Most of them are pathetic. Time marches on.

The Rack Boy's final achievement remains unequalled. I didn't witness it, but the cops arrested him one night for drunken driving. Nothing exceptional, you say? Usually not, but The Rack Boy couldn't drive. Indeed, he didn't own a car. Never had.

How then, I hear you say? Well, a local Thug encountered The Rack Boy in a beer hall one night and offered him a ride home. So the Rack Boy crawled into the back seat and promptly passed out. The Thug forgot he was there and headed for his own house. On the way he amused himself by pinging fenders of parked cars on either side of the street. He finally misjudged his angle and crashed into one of those parked cars.

Lights came on behind the Thug, indicating citizen concerns. So the Thug got out and walked home.

When the police arrived, they couldn't find a driver; all they could find was The Rack Boy, still passed out in the back seat. They didn't know what exactly to do, so they arrested him and took him in. I heard they got it all straightened out eventually and released The Rack Boy on his own recognizance. This event soon became a legend among the beer guzzlers in that little town. I first heard about it from The Brother, but the Rack Boy never fessed up. He rarely seemed embarrassed, but I think that incident got to him.

The Junior Year

By the time my junior year rolled around the townies had pretty much accepted me, which seemed mighty important to me at the time. I didn't do athletics, to be sure, (except for snooker) but they considered me a good actor and a whiz-bang in the science classes.

All this led me to pursue my number one priority: girls. As opposed to the one passable female in grade school, this place had girls out the wazoo, one might say. I began to try to cut one or more out of the herd.

Various opportunities arose. Saturday nights one of the local churches held a dance for high school types, known far and wide as "The Episcopalian Belly-Rub." A guy could shuffle around for a couple of hours with assorted girls, then try to maneuver his heart's desire to his car, if he had one. Car, that is. If not, tough luck, but one could improvise, and one had friends, after all.

Some of the younger lady scholars seemed to bat their eyes as I passed by, but by then I had learned in the pool hall about laws prohibiting underage sex, and those young ladies constituted what we called jail bait. That wouldn't have stopped me, given the chance, but I lacked a copulation location. When I got my car, Pontiac's 1929 clone of the Model T Ford, it would have made in-car frolics a study in Zen acrobatics. It would have required more cooperation from the female of the species than either they or I dreamed possible.

My terror and ignorance compounded the problems.

I once had eyes for A Catholic Virgin, a tasty morsel I'd met in church. Even then I intuited that she belonged to that most admirable subspecies of humanity, Dirty Girls. I don't know if she ever reached her potential, and I didn't know how to lead her there, so I only got to kiss her on the cheek. Once. Oh, be still, my beating heart! And be still, my throbbing . . . well, never mind. I gave up on her in due course as a lost cause. The first of many.

But my cause célèbre during these years was The Breed. So called because her father came from Spain; not, she hastened to point out, Mexico, but Spain. Her mother taught art locally, so The Breed knew everything; art, classical music, books, a true sophisticate.

She had no truck with high school boys, she once told a friend of mine, except for one. Me. I blushed becomingly and tugged my forelock.

One of our frottage sessions took place not parked on a road but by the coal shed at The Country Grade School. After we'd been to a movie, as I recall. Alas, we both fell asleep, in all honesty. Waking up to The Breed telling me she had to get home and finding the car battery dead constituted one of the low points in my life, up to that point.

We could do nothing except walk the two miles to my home, The Little House on the Prairie, Part Three, wake up The Father, and ask him to drive us over and give my car a push to get started. I would then return The Breed to her domicile, and drive, slowly, very damned slowly, back home.

No one confronted me when I arrived, so I crept into my bed and tried to sleep. When I arose for breakfast The Mother began firing broadsides. Did I not realize that I was under some sort of sacred trust when I took out a young lady? Did I not realize the damage that could be done to her reputation as well as mine? And what led me to take her to the coal shed that late, anyway?

I explained that The Breed wanted to see where I had gone to grade school, so I took her out to see it, and we both fell asleep. Certainly no one could blame either of us.

Thin, very thin. True, though.

The Father, who had kept silent during this Inquisition, as usual had the last word. As he left for the barn and the morning milking of the cow-brutes, he paused a moment at the door.

"How did she *like* the school house?"

Having thrown jet fuel on the flames, he went to tend to the cattle. I crammed some food down my neck and escaped as soon as possible, and eventually the matter faded into the distance.

The Breed and I broke up during my senior year, to the delight of my buddies.

Other Janie-Come-Latelies appeared for brief episodes of no real significance. One of the local round heels, a faculty daughter, come to think of it, introduced me to French kissing when she tried to lick my tonsils one evening. No one had warned me about this, but I learned quickly in those days given half a chance.

Classes in My Junior Year

I became a solid B student. The junior year curriculum for those of us bound for college began with a half credit of Constitution. Taught by the basketball coach, this one semester course should have made informed citizens of us all, at least the ones who stayed out of jail. I endured it.

For the second semester, lest we just wander about, happy as clouds, the debate coach taught Psychology at us. I remember rationalization as an interesting concept. Beyond that, nothing. Nada.

Advanced Algebra followed. I'd done geometry the year before, but I don't remember Advanced Algebra in the least. I took my C and went to:

Chemistry was my best thing, besides acting. There my light shone like a super nova and I left the jocks writhing in the dust, but they clustered around me during examinations. The relatively young teacher, recently licensed to instruct us, taught strictly from the textbook.

Of course, the book contained egregious errors, leading me to realize that something printed could be utterly wrong. For example, the text assured us matter could not be converted to energy nor vice versa, just not possible. This was some years after explosions in Alamogordo, Hiroshima, and Nagasaki had proven otherwise. I wondered about this, but I kept my mouth shut and answered exam questions along the establishment lines. Had I corrected the book my colleagues would have drawn and quartered me or forced me into the agriculture classes in Basic, Intermediate, and Advanced Hog Guts.

One would-be jock assigned himself to me as a lab partner, assuming that he might pass the course that way, which he did. He also dragged my hand into a Bunsen burner flame one day, causing me to flip a dilute solution of hydrochloric acid into my eyes. The teacher, fully trained for such emergencies, stuck my head into the waste sink at the end of the lab table and flushed me, hell, damned near drowned me, with floods of water. Later an MD checked me out and pronounced me good to go.

Some benefits accrued, however; my lab partner assumed the position of campaign manager for my run at the Senior Class presidency. While talk arose of false ballot counting, dishonesty in general, and such, I won that lofty post fair and nearly square.

But Chemistry challenged me not in the least; I aced it with no trouble. The teacher one day took a short piece of glass tubing, fused one end in a burner, and then blew a small bubble on it. He told us to give it a try, leading to a number of burned fingers and curses.

Being a smart ass, of course, I used a trick The Brother taught me and blew a bubble on both ends of my glass tube. I then handed it to the teacher, who admitted he had not the remotest idea of how I'd done it. Nor did any of the other witless wonders in the class.

It's not all that tough; you fuse one end of a tube and blow a bubble as usual. After letting it cool, then you fuse the other end and pass the first bubble quickly through the burner's flame. The heat expands the air in the first bubble, thereby creating a second bubble on the other end. Let it cool down, present it to the teacher, and hope he doesn't get honked off about it. Then take your place among the Immortals.

One might wonder why I didn't enter myself in the state high school scholarship contests. After all, I had placed third in the state in General Science my freshman year. So why didn't I take my chemical awareness to the contests? I have no idea; I suppose the state still held such contests. Or maybe I spent too much time speculating at girls.

After Chemistry I wandered off to a class in Beginning Spanish. I'd have taken French, but the school didn't offer it. I'm not even sure why I took Spanish; college prep courses required a language, yes, but I'd had two years of Latin. I may have needed a few more hours to graduate.

So there I was. The Spanish Teacher seemed a decent sort of person. She was one of my first experiences with a teacher who actually liked to teach, who felt honored to be able to share her enthusiasm for her subject with her students. That seemed to me a requirement for good teaching, but I found few persons so blessed. From first grade through a doctorate I remember a half dozen at best.

The Spanish Teacher also gave me something I'd never had before: an assignment to teach a class all by myself. She went to a state teachers' convention of some sort, which I suppose gave her a chance to get away and run wild. She didn't have any teaching assistants, so she converted me into one. I took it seriously. The Spanish teacher handed me a lesson plan, assignment sheets, an answer sheet to some tests, bade me *vaya con dios* and went to her convention.

I had two good buddies in that class; I took them aside and assured them I would kick them in the crotch till they bled if they didn't back my play. They went along with it. True, one of them spent most of that time grabbing at Jean the Machine, but I didn't blame him for that; I had eyes for that one myself.

We proceeded on.

GYM. One last semester of gym in the fall and English in the spring rounded out my junior year. Gym class was a farce at best; I avoided working up a sweat with no trouble at all. I would get swatted on the butt from time to time by the teacher, but it didn't really hurt.

ENGLISH. I have little memory of Junior English, but one event in there I will always remember, yea, unto my deathbed. Our teacher, well-meaning but misled, read aloud to us every damned word of *A Tale of Two Cities*. She never told us why we had to endure this. We paid little attention to it and did homework for other classes during this marathon; it bored the dickens out of us. I suppose she thought it was an example of excellence in literature, but she'd have done better with Mickey Spillane.

I got my B, anyway.

Yearbooks

Every spring the Journalism class prepared yearbooks. I still have the first three paperbacks, but they had converted to hardback covers for my senior year. Of course, they bristled with misspellings, duplicate entries, omissions, and blurred photographs. But the school scheduled an evening for everyone in Senior High to assemble in the boys' gym to sign one another's yearbooks.

I had to obliterate some of my messages; they might have held up in court. Some, indeed, most, said only "good luck to a swell kid," that sort of imaginative thing. Some offered diatribes against particular teachers. Some guys filled their notes with sexual remarks of the crudest sort, and these I hid from The Parental Units.

But the yearbooks gave us a record of a sort; for whatever reasons I kept mine all these sixty-plus years and have them yet. As I approach death and transfiguration I think I will return them to dust and ashes, lest surviving family members have too much fun reading them. I think nothing in there would still constitute grounds for litigation; if they haven't caught me in sixty-six years, I think I made a clean getaway.

Athletics

I think I might have enjoyed being on the track team, at least before I started smoking, but I didn't know we had a track team. Football, basketball, and tennis remained total mysteries; I had not the foggiest idea how to play any of them.

But to flaunt our butchness five or six of us would get to the local college gym during our high school basketball games. We always secured front row seats. Our mighty pep band roosted in the top bleachers and bleated out various fight songs for which no one knew the words.

Our team competed with schools from neighboring towns, including a Big Town to the north, which had a whole bunch of high schools in it. Big Town North, Big Town East, and so on. The Big Town schools actually had black players, and eventually so did we. Black cagers were a novelty, but no one denied how well they performed. Crude racial taunts often greeted them, I fear. Shameful, and they would get your clock cleaned nowadays, but times change. Sometimes they even get better. It can happen.

Our high school fielded pretty mediocre teams, occasionally scoring an upset but never as I recall winning a championship at anything. Cheerleaders exhorted us, "We gotta win! We gotta win!" but even then, I thought to myself, no, we don't *have* to win. The sun will come up tomorrow.

The cheerleaders whooped it up immediately in front of us, the most popular girls in the school flaunting short skirts with matching panties and unfortunately heavy sweaters. We applauded them with vigor and rated them from one to ten.

We had a player named Dan, and another cheer went "Booger Dan, he's our man! If he can't do it, no one can." I never learned how he got that nickname, but I really didn't want to know.

Other than basketball the only sport we actually attended was football, played on the local college field on Friday nights. Cheap lighting barely illuminated the field. Again, we rarely won anything. The only game I recall is the one during which I went to the top of the stadium and lobbed a dead squirrel into the crowd. It landed in a middle-aged lady's lap. She got up and did a little dance, never witnessed in that part of the country before, including her banshee imitation.

Our powerhouse football team won two, lost six, and tied one. The B Squad, on the other hand, won four and lost only one, astonishing one and all. I suppose that inspired them to arrange their hands so as to shoot the bird to the photographer for the team photo. These shots escaped the notice of the teeny-bopper editors and survive to this day.

The basketball team, however, placed fourth in the state. During the entire season the most points they scored was 54, the least 31. Different times, those.

ASIDE: This bird-shooting tradition by jocks dates at least as far back as 1884, when the immortal baseball pitcher, Charles "Old Hoss" Radbourne, shot the first photographed bird as a member of the Providence Grays. He's in the Baseball Hall of Fame, but not for bird-shooting.

And the dust jacket of Edward Acorn's excellent biography, Fifty-nine in '84, has a photo of Old Hoss flipping off the world. The title refers to Old Hoss winning fifty-nine (some say sixty) games that season. You could look it up.

Other teams amassed lackluster records, but we paid little attention to track, tennis, wrestling, baseball, and such like. We had achieved a level of sophistication hitherto undreamed of in The High School, no doubt about it.

I watched a tennis match or two, but I had no concept of good versus bad in that game. Some dudes from The Local Junior College had painted "WEENIE SUCKERS" in enamel on our courts. Charming, but I guess our janitors didn't have the right stuff to eradicate it.

The Senior Year

Well, we'd made it. We strutted around as Lords of Creation for our final year. As Class President I chaired a few meetings and led discussions of our various social events. True, thc class neglected to tell me about one meeting; they held it during Home Room period and the entire class showed up, less me. They decided if I couldn't make it they would put the vice president in charge. Unfortunately, he and I had sneaked out to shoot snooker during Home Room, but my main squeeze, The Breed, called The Pool Hall Downtown and convinced us to return. We got a nice round of applause when we appeared, but not from the faculty.

The class decided on "Under the Sea" as a banquet theme. Some higher authority should outlaw that theme immediately and permanently.

I note from my transcript that I had only three and a half courses in the senior year. I don't know how that happened or what I did with the extra free time. Studied, most likely. And also snookered.

Senior days began with American History, taught by the aging sponsor of the Senior Class, a pleasant if stern lady. I somehow extracted a grade of B from American History. I spent a lot of time adding graffiti to the textbook illustrations. We rented our texts, no one bought them. We had done the same in grade school; I went to college before I actually bought and owned textbooks. That imposition cut deeply into my pitiful budget.

American History, the first class of the day, also included Home Room. After the administration brought us up to date, we devoted the extra time to study and thinking deep thoughts.

Next came Physics, taught by an older male teacher who also coached tennis quite well. He expected me to emulate The Brother, who had excelled under his tutelage, but I offered only sore disappointments. Since Physics contained nothing all that difficult I escaped with another gentlemanly B. I might have done better, but after reading Robert Heinlein I offered to build a fourth dimensional hypercube for the class; the teacher didn't see much need for it. Or for me, for that matter. He thought I was just wasting my time. Looking back, he was right.

I should have breezed through Dramatics, taught by the new teacher of such things. She didn't moon over me like the one who left to get married, and I got yet another B.

My last high school course was Physiology. A one-semester course in which I got my final B. I don't remember who taught it, if we had a text, what we did, or a damned thing about it. Surely it contained no sex education; the high school complied with the prevailing social trends of the day, keep them ignorant as long as possible. Let them find their own way. Teach them how to drive cars, but not how to make babies. Did they ever suspect we might try to combine those two activities?

So there we had it. Seventeen and a half credits of College Prep courses, then the high school spat me out to seek my amusements elsewhere. Before that, however, we had a couple of rituals traditional to senior classes. Clichés, to be sure, but not to us; we hadn't done them before. I don't know who told us about them, but someone did. That high school wasn't always there, so someone had to start these traditions, but no one seems to know who. Whoever created the practice probably ended up either in politics or the penitentiary. Possibly both. But we eagerly went along with them, since everyone we knew urged us to do so, and they sounded like fun and a way to express our imagined superiority.

The Senior Sneak

Sometime in late spring the conspiracy arose among the seniors to take a day off. We played hooky that day and partied ourselves to a standstill. Wc first drove around the school, honking like demented geese, then took off for various venues. I don't know where others went, but my happy little band crossed a nearby border into another state. There we had a picnic, but, more importantly, most of the boys got themselves around some drinkin' whiskey.

Most of us enjoyed beer on occasion, but we had trouble getting the hard stuff. Older friends found bootleggers and obtained the goods, though. Southern Comfort, as I recall, a sickly, sweet bourbon. They thought they did us a favor.

So we found a city park and unloaded. The picnic went as picnics usually do, but then the bottles made the rounds. The girls did not partake, but the boys all wanted to show their manliness by swilling a batch. For most it was the first time.

The Sneak soon became a contest to see who could get the drunkest. Chugging hard liquor is not wise for teen-agers, as some of us soon discovered. But we left our problems behind us in piles in that city's park, and the girls drove us back to town, by which time we had somewhat sobered up.

In due course we discovered that all our parents, the high school teachers and staff, and several others knew all about our little outing. We had a tattletale in our class but couldn't find him. Or her. Or them.

High school seniors all over the country enjoyed this tradition for years. In some primitive societies the elders would have circumcised us, boys and girls alike. Sneak Day seemed preferable, I think.

But we had all sobered up in time for our last hurrah, at which time all sins would be forgiven.

Graduation

As class president I led the march in to the traditional "Pomp and Circumstance," blatted out by juniors and sophomores. I also gave a brief speech, which the class sponsor later said she loved. She should have; she wrote it. The class sang, although it wasn't on the program, "So Long, It's Been Good to Know You," as well as "Good Night, Irene," a few of my buddies adding, "You Sex Machine!" The top grade-getters spoke briefly, as well. The crowd endured it; The Parents gave me a wristwatch dubbed "The Academy Award," and high school ground to a halt. Not a moment too soon.

Pre-College Summer Vacation

Summer yawned before me, three months of no education whatsoever except what I read on my own or found in The Pool Hall.

Two summers earlier The Father decided he'd had enough of my lolling around the house all day reading who knew what filth. I took a job with the local Coca-Cola bottling operation. Six ten-hour days a week they worked me, at forty cents an hour. That comes to $24 a week; I don't recall if they deducted tax or social security, but I obtained a social security card, which I still have around here somewhere.

I lasted two weeks bottling Cokes. I hated the interruption of my reading program. The boss said I was the laziest worker he had ever enslaved, so that didn't help. Once I sat in front of a bank of florescent lights while freshly filled Cokes went by on a conveyor belt. They theorized that I would detect any impurities in the bottles: mice, nails, chewing gum, insects, whatever. In practice, however, the flickering light and dark only succeeded in hypnotizing me while unthinkable debris went out for public consumption. The boss relieved me of that duty, as well as any others.

I didn't drink another Coke for several years. I knew too much.

The next summer I worked for the City as part of a crew of three maintaining a large old cemetery. Mostly we mowed the grass and clipped the hedges. I soon found a way to screw that up, too; I ran one of the mowers across a gravel road without turning it off or raising the blade. Said blade picked up a piece of gravel and shot it into my ankle at very high speed indeed, necessitating a visit to the doctor. I hoped to be released from duty, but the M.D. sent me back to the trenches.

The cemetery was almost full, but still had available a few plots owned by elderly locals. If one of them snuffed it, we three dug him or her a grave. We used pick and shovels, long before the days of back hoes or jack hammers or anything that would make the work easier. And while the ceremony went on the three of us lolled around just out of sight, often playing pitch, a rummy game of utter simplicity. My compatriots, the boss and a fellow helot, couldn't play pitch any better than they could sing grand opera, so I managed to enhance my income a bit. When the ceremony ended we moseyed over and filled in the grave.

When it rained we stayed in the tool shed, getting paid and playing more pitch. That suited me just fine.

The cemetery turned out to be a marvelous place to park with girls, too. The poor little dears would marvel at my courage for working in a place like that and seek solace in my arms. A little bit of solace, at any rate.

But this summer, as a high school graduate, The City offered me a different, better job. And, indeed, I rather enjoyed the assignment, and it paid better.

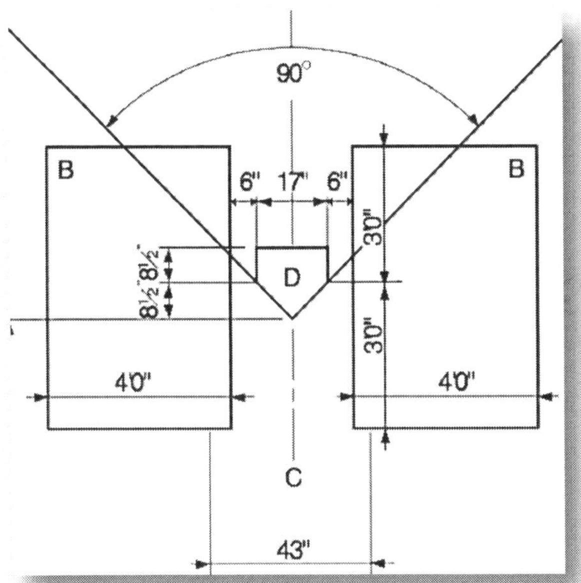

Dimensions involved in a baseball batter's box. A template helped, but I had to go look this up the first time I laid it out. The defense rests. From the author's collection.

For that summer I oversaw and maintained the municipal baseball park. Before evening games I'd put out the bases and chalk the assorted lines and the batter's box. The City supplied me a sort of template, made of 1" x 3" boards, for the batter's box, but I had no clear notion of what relation it had, geographical wise, to home plate. I didn't want to ask; that might blow the whole bit. Musing on this for a while, I stalked into the City Library and demanded an encyclopedia, in which I looked up "baseball" and found the appropriate dimensions. Well, I didn't know them. Do you?

It's a better than even money bet that the next baseball fan you meet won't know the dimensions in question.

I couldn't quit after I had prepared the field; I had to remain on the grounds, amuse myself as fate and imagination would have it during the baseball, then bring in the bases and turn off the lights after the game. My working day thus covered my time from about three in the afternoon, unless the field needed mowing, to perhaps nine or ten at night. Three to nine is six hours, but I received pay for eight, meager though it was.

Not many girls came to the city league ball games, but I kept an eye out for them. The lighting did not encourage reading, so I climbed up into what passed for a press box, a rickety frame structure about ten feet high, with a public address system, a desk, and a few chairs. The local newspaper sent a high school kid every evening to cover the games and announce the lineups. He loved being a reporter but hated using the PA system. I offered him a deal whereby I would announce the lineups and changes and such, although I didn't know squat about baseball and regularly amused the crowd with my goofs. I didn't much care; I discovered I could get paid while sitting down, and my whole world changed once again.

As it turned out the City paid me more just to hang around the ballpark than he got for reporting on the games. He eventually wrote a history of that city league, but he didn’t even mention me. Strange.

So that completed my getaway from The Little House on the Prairie, Part Three; The Country Grade School; The Little Town Nearby' and The High School. That autumn I headed north, riding with a friend, with a suitcase, a few dollars for tuition, and not much more.

By God, I had made my escape, getting over the hills and out of sight into a land of more mixed blessings than I could handle.

Many more. Many, many more.

But they weren't all blessings.

<u>CHAPTER SEVEN</u>

COLLEGE JOYS, OR, STUPID IS AS STUPID DOES

I really didn't want to write this chapter. I didn't want to relive or reveal my utter and total stupidity—academic, social, financial, etc. When I left high school and headed out with a glad cry I had high hopes for a new life at The Teachers College. Two years later, dazed, whimpering, bewildered, mortified, embarrassed, whipped, and ashamed, I crept back home, to the farm I had so longed to leave.

Freshman Orientation

You see, I had no more business in college than I had in a *corps de ballet*. I learned that I didn't actually have to go to class, so I didn't, very often, if they didn't amuse me, and not many of them did.

I paid my tuition, $54.00. Not per credit hour, $54.00 for the entire semester with a class load of fifteen hours. True, these were 1951 prices, but I guess they knew the value of their product at The Teachers College.

They still give me a call or a letter now and again, asking for money. For God's sake, they trained us to be public school teachers and now they want money? It is to snigger and guffaw, and also to chortle and giggle.

New freshmen had to take a course called Freshman Orientation. All the newbies gathered once a week in a large auditorium to learn about college. One of the first things we learned was we had to wear a beany. Most of the girls found that just too utterly cute, but the boys thought them effeminate and demeaning. Packs of lettermen prowled the campus, hunting down freshmen without beanies. These jocks carried paddles to swat the buttocks of any guy without his beany. I never saw them whack any girls, tempting as it must have been. Some of us (me) claimed to be transfer students, which confused the jocks and got us off the hook.

I don't recall that Freshman Orientation oriented us toward anything that we needed to know; it was pretty much a waste of time. We learned that girls had "hours," and that meant that if they lived in a dorm or a sorority they had to be back in it by ten or ten-thirty, or something like that. If they weren't back they got locked out and had to wake up the guards to let them in, guards who would give them demerits. Weekends had slightly more liberal hours, but not much. Those regulations didn't do the least bit of good, of course. Well, they did somewhat increase the attraction factor of the townies and the girls who lived off campus. Sure did. Yup.

Sororities and Fraternities

Early in the fall term the fraternities and sororities began their membership drives. One could, if found acceptable, become a "pledge" in a Greek organization for a semester. After that came an initiation and the pledge thus became an active, or full member. The frat boys sold us the myth that we'd become a happy band of brothers, making friendships that would endure the rest of our lives. Sure we would. The check's in the mail. I'm here from to government to help you.

I'd make bigger mistakes in my life than pledging a fraternity, but I'd put it on my short list. First of all, I had no more in common with a house full of jocks than I did with the Home

Economics Club. They talked jock talk constantly, and a few of us gave not a damn for that.

To illustrate the level of sophistication among the jocks I recall one lout who proposed to marry a young lady he'd been courting for months. As he put it, "if you've been going with her for six months and haven't laid her, you might as well marry her, because that's going to be some *good* pussy!"

His fraternity brothers nodded wisely in agreement. My doubts began to grow about the entire fraternal concept.

The fraternity insisted that pledges move into the frat house so they could keep an eye on us, so I did just that. Another mistake. We had crummy beds (army surplus, I suspect), a communal bathroom, and mashed potatoes for dinner most nights. Lots of mashed potatoes. Lunches we had to find on our own. An elderly lady called a "house mother" oversaw the entire operation, without whom the frats would have descended into total anarchy. Think *Animal House.* We were close to that. Weekends we spent gambling and drinking; I don't recall ever seeing one of my Greek brothers open a book. They may have sneaked off to do that, I don't know. Some said the campus contained a library, but they weren't sure just where it was.

An interesting if pathetic event was the frequent return of a certain ex-fraternity member; we'll call him Fred. Apparently, Fred thought his frat days represented the high point of his life, so he came back often. I have no idea what he did or where he lived, but he would show up on Saturdays. He'd get liquored up with some of the rest of us, and spend the evening playing and singing "St. James Infirmary" over and over on a beat-up old piano. I loved that song, but that was about all of value I got from my fraternal experience.

One of the more pleasant aspects of pledge status, other than binge drinking, consisted of the Pledge Sneak, when we all stole off to some off-campus site to booze ourselves commode-hugging, grass-grabbing drunk, pledge eternal friendship, and tell monstrous lies. The actives all put up with this since they knew their turn would come.

Hell Week

Eventually the fall semester ended with "Hell Week," the initiation designed to take us from pledge status to active. First, we had to prove our raging desire to elevate ourselves to the brotherhood by suffering through the most idiotic and humiliating things the actives could dream up.

"Hell Week" would have fascinated the Marquis de Sade. Actually, he may have invented it as a party game. It seemed to be a master plan to rid the pledge class of any dignity, rather like a hospital. None of us quit, though; if my comrades could put up with it, so could I. I still wonder what would have happened if one of us had told the actives to go pound rocks up their butts. But none of us had that much moxie. We wanted liberation, true, but we also craved to belong. That's a hard pair to draw to.

So we all endured group humiliations, the details of which I will not describe. Suffice to say we all got naked and underwent various humiliations. After all that fun ended, the actives drove us, still naked, a few miles out of town and dumped us out on a country road. Then they told us to get back to the frat house as best we could.

We got back, God knows how. I not only got back, and got to be an active member, but I also got pneumonia and had to return to the family farm for rest and rehabilitation. I deserved it for being a schmuck and putting up with such nonsense. I should have remained an independent, and before long I was indeed just that. I had rather willingly wasted two years of my college career, as some called it. This did not sit well with anyone: The Parents, deans, faculty, The Sibs, my friends on campus, my friends back home, and most of all, most seriously of all, my own self. Failure is hardly ever fun.

Life as an Active

We received our pins from our brothers at a candle-lit ceremony; we learned the secret handshake, and all that, and we went forth as full-fledged studs.

I didn't last long, though. I made it through the spring semester after I got back from the pneumonia, but with diminishing enthusiasm for fraternal functions. The next autumn my brothers excoriated me for not sitting with them in the Student Union instead of joining my friends from the theatre department. They fussed at me for a while until I returned my pin and split the blanket with them for good.

That was over sixty years ago, but I'll be damned if I don't still get mailings requesting contributions to the group. Beyond belief. That's carrying fraternalism too far.

As for making friends I would have all my life, I did just that during those two years, but none from the fraternity. I sort of kept in touch with one of the frat brothers, a poet, of all things, but he passed from the scene recently. How and why he joined that frat I'll never know, but he was from Nebraska.

A couple of my would-be life-long brothers tried to pick fights with me. The first one had lost a leg in a car wreck in high school, and I really didn't know how or why to fight a one-legged guy. I wondered how he, during Hell Week, got his naked body back to the fraternity house on one leg. Maybe the actives let him keep his wooden leg.

The other one had both legs, but he was even stupider than I was. I ridiculed them both and no fights took place. Violence is the last resort of an exhausted mentality, and these two dudes wore out their gray matter in kindergarten, as near as I could tell.

Classes

Thank God I don't have a transcript from my first two years at The Teachers College. I would hate reliving those awful years and recording how completely retarded I was. It wasn't that I couldn't have handled the academic load; it just never occurred to me to try. I'd always gotten by in classes by native cunning without bothering to read the texts or anything foolish like that. Alas, those days had vanished. We were supposed to play hardball in college, not like high school.

In my first two years of college I accumulated, on a 3.0 scale, a Grade Point Average of 0.8. That's zero point eight. Naught dot eight. Pitiful. Embarrassing. Putrid. Disgusting. Beneath contempt. Appalling.

I wouldn't have gotten the few points I did if I hadn't taken the required set of English courses, including World Literature. In one of those courses we read *Hamlet, Prince of Denmark*. Well, hell, I'd already read that, so I breezed through that unit. I'd read it a couple of times; I even knew who Reynaldo was. He's in there, I swear. You could look it up.

In World Literature I found another masterpiece, Dante's *Divine Comedy*. Or at least the first part of it, *The Inferno*. I thought for several years that *The Inferno* constituted the entirety of *The Divine Comedy* but then discovered the other two parts and tried them. Not a patch on *The Inferno*.

Dorothy Sayers, an accomplished and highly regarded scholar, did the translation we read. Years later I discovered she earned tidy sums writing mysteries, but I never read any of them. I finally tried one. I think I'll probably just stick with Sherlock Holmes and Spenser.

A bust of Dante. It cost more than I wanted to pay. He even made Hell pretty entertaining, at least to those just passing through. I could dig it. Photo by the author.

Years later while moseying down a street in Florence, Italy, I came upon a sign saying, "Dante's House." I immediately went in to see a sort of miniature museum of no great import, but I grew a bit closer to Dante. He was an oasis in another otherwise bleak desert of my own making. To be sure, I didn't believe a word he said about Hell, Purgatory, or Heaven; I'd heard all that before. But I liked his style.

A Few Uppers

The high point of my first two years at The Teachers College came while I dozed in Personal Finance, another required course. I was jolted awake and thought someone had kicked my chair, but I was sitting in the back row. It seems a small earthquake had happened. Unmitigated prairie for hundreds of miles in every direction and we get an earthquake? Well, when you go out of town sometimes people treat you bad.

Another positive experience at The Teachers College came when I took Astronomy. When I entered the college, they gave me a series of tests, and if I did well on them they would excuse me from the usual required basic courses. They adjudicated me as exempt from biology, math, and general science, which didn't surprise me especially. What did surprise me was that I had to take advanced courses in each of those subjects.

So I hunted down an advisor and wondered WTF. He said I could take calculus. I asked what calculus was; I'd never heard of it. When I couldn't get a straight answer out of him, nor anyone else, I thanked them and signed up for Astronomy, also in the Math Department because they didn't know where else to put it. Physics would have made more sense.

In that class I again found for one of the few times in my life a teacher who seemed to think God had blessed him to share his enthusiasm for his subject with his students. Indeed, in that regard he reminded me of that Spanish teacher back at The High School. I dug the cosmic scene hard, but the math majors in the class seemed to find the universe a bore. Being under the influence of the science fiction I had read, I eagerly tried to absorb as much of the cosmos as I could. Most of what I learned by then has been disproved or updated, but none of us knew what was coming.

The class had regular evening meetings in a pasture to gape at celestial wonders through a telescope. At least those of us who stayed gaped; most of the rest wandered off to a nearby beer hall or started making out behind some convenient bushes.

I wanted to turn the telescope toward the girls' dorm, but the prof wouldn't hear of it. But I remember him fondly; he even approved of my term paper on sundials. So what if what he taught us is now no longer true; it was then. As I keep telling my relatives, truth is relative. Well, that's my theory, and I'm sticking to it.

Other Stuff

I took other courses, or for the most part they took me. I lacked the smarts to absorb knowledge by osmosis; I had to read the textbooks. But I didn't. So I failed several courses, one of which I repeated, only to get a grade of D the second time around. And that course's prof sponsored my fraternity. So much for brotherhood. He didn't like me, and I sure as hell had no partiality for him.

I should add The College required gym courses; they had not yet abolished that foolishness. We scholars cavorted around in our cute little shorts, same as in high school. But I found one course I loved: Archery. The football coach taught it, sort of; he didn't have a clue. I did well, since I'd learned some archery in Boy Scout camp. But it became evident that a wart hog could pass through the eye of a needle more easily than a Speech and Theatre major could get an A in a Physical Education course. The same thing happened in Boxing I; I only got hit once, when I tried to do a triple fake against an old country boy. He missed all three fakes and floored me. But when the grades came out I once again scored a B.

Sometimes, they just don't play fair in the big leagues.

The entire Teachers College experience dissolved into a mess. Professors regularly berated me for goofing off. Both Deans (they had one for women and one for men) took me aside and spoke to me. Why they banned me from the women's dorm I didn't understand; I'd never been in it. I still haven't, for that matter.

Actually, my first two years of college, miserable as they were, had some long-term benefits. As a professor during the Viet Nam War I could show male students my transcript and urge them to continue in their college career. They gazed on my grades in horror, but I think they decided that if their professor could overcome total worthlessness, so could they. One kid sent me a note, thanking me for saving his life by keeping him out of Nam where people would have shot at him and very possibly have killed him. They say it's an ill wind, etc., and I suppose it might be. I don't recall how he happened to get an acceptable grade in whatever course it was, but I had begun to consider grades as low priority.

Big-time Show Biz

I thought I was an actor; I had been in high school, after all. And was accounted a good actor, like Polonius. So I hung out at the theatre and eventually the Department hired me on to work on the stage crew, building scenery. This paid $50 a month, and The Parents sent me another fifty bucks monthly, and that's what I tried to live on. It was all I could scrape up in those bygone days.

On that stage crew I did indeed make some friends that I've kept the rest of my days. Many of them have passed on to that Great Green Room in the Sky, where I will join them some day and split a beer. They were a raucous crew, really; drinking and smoking up a storm. We had only heard of the killer weed, marijuana, but we'd have tried it if we could have found some. The State was still dry, so the crew and I had to make do with 3.2 percent beer, Later liquor stores became legal and we moved up to the hard stuff, which we couldn't handle at first. We hung in there, though, and got the hang of it; we were nothing if not diligent, if only in matters of intoxicants.

Theatre parties happened all over the county. After the Saturday night performance we would take a garbage can filled with ice and beer to the city dump. About dawn our chief light technician slowly mimed fading in the sunrise on an imaginary set of dimmers. These booze-ups we called Dawnbusters, and I remember them fondly, even if they shot Sundays all to hell and gone. Sunday evening we'd show up for a rehearsal of the next show and the entire cycle would begin again. Eight shows we would do over the course of the summer; two directors sharing the load. Usually one show was a musical of some sort, which about did us in. They're hard.

Parties took place in various apartments rented by theatre majors. Not everyone attended, but the hard core (a term chosen advisedly) of the theatre gang usually took part. We'd drink more beer. For a few years we would read aloud from the comic strip "Pogo, the Possum," and have great fun with that. Cartoonist Walt Kelly even wrote our favorite Christmas carol:

Deck us all with Boston Charlie,
Walla Walla, Wash., an' Kalamazoo!
Nora's freezin' on the trolley,
Swaller dollar cauliflower alley-garoo!

The departmental directors cast me in a couple of shows, usually as some sort of robotic store dummy. I could not relax on stage, and I wonder now why I wanted to act like an actor. But I did, and I became a part of the group. Eventually I became better at it. Sophisticated comedy performed by farm kids who'd never been out of the state must have been hard to take, but I don't think our audiences were much hipper. At least they said they liked our work, and who were we to argue? We had the attraction, at least, of being somewhat live.

I had lots of fun those first two years, oh, my, yes, I did, but none of it had to do with Grade Point Averages. The thought of graduating never crossed my mind. I spent my time just carping the diem all day long and into the nights.

Moving Up to Factory Work

After four semesters of making a complete ass of myself I left The Teachers College. No one on that campus tried to slow me down as I vanished over the horizon, so I just slunk out of town and crept home, more than a little crestfallen.

The first thing I needed was a job, of course, although I had every intention of joining the Navy, following The Brother's example. But first I looked for a job. I didn't try to get back on with the City in cemeteries or ballparks, though.

My best shot was to work in a crayon factory in my hometown in a structure that looked more like a campus than a sweatshop. I applied, they hired me, and I made about as much money as possible locally. Quite a bit better than the Coca-Cola bottling plant, at least.

On the job in work clothes I felt the vague suspicion that I had somehow lost the way; I had gone wrong.

The foreman introduced me to a machine called a mold and a guy who operated it. These molds produced a whole pile of crayons about every five minutes, and the operator had to inspect and then put them in a wooden box and stack the box on a pallet before the next lot emerged. He didn't have a whole lot of time to fool around; the pace of the mold and the pace of the operator matched pretty nicely. On a good eight-hour day this cycle could be repeated anywhere from eighty to a hundred times. That was a hell of a lot of crayons, to be sure; our plant supplied many little nippers, indeed.

I learned quickly. A steam-heated vat by each mold contained melted wax and pigment, which the operator poured into the mold using buckets. While the wax cooled, the operator flipped the last bunch of crayons onto a table against a backdrop and inspected them for flaws, like bad points. Imperfections went back into the tank for another try.

As a molder I would hit a couple of buttons and produce my wooden box full of crayons twelve times an hour. When the stack contained eighteen boxes, a guy on a forklift hauled it off to the labelers. The labeled crayons were then fed into machines that put them in boxes. After that they went into shipping cartons and disappeared into the warehouse, then out into the Great Beyond, which in our case was the real estate between the Mississippi River and the Rocky Mountains.

Women operated the labeling machines. The molders ogled the ladies as they bent over to pick up boxes of crayons, and if one bent over facing away from the molders, a barrage of crayons would pop her on the bum.

A counter on the mold kept track of the output. The foreman checked it every afternoon to see that workers weren't goofing off more than usual.

We had a half-hour brown bag lunch break, during which I learned that the molders were mainly farmers who couldn't make a living farming. We used the break to discuss baseball and politics at a childish level, appropriate for a crayon factory. One guy was a token Democrat who admitted to me that he was only a Democrat to piss off everyone else in that hotbed of conservatism.

After a week or so the administration started a night shift to fill the increasing demand from little kiddies in kindergarten and grade schools. They invited me to make crayons on this shift, working seven hours but getting paid for eight, four p.m. to eleven. The discussions over dinner break were a trifle more sophisticated than the day crew's but not much. I didn't care.

I soon decided being controlled by a machine, responding to flashing lights, wasn't an attractive way of life for me. So once again I plotted a getaway. Another young molder and I found amusements where we could. We enlisted the assistance of a labeling machine lady, first of all. Then from time to time we might slip notes into crayon boxes, usually reading "Help me, I'm a prisoner in a crayon factory, oh, please help me!" No one ever responded, nor was there ever trouble because we'd slipped a competitor's crayon into a box of ours before they shipped.

Now it came to pass that this company operated three factories, one back east, one on the West Coast, and ours. The eastern factory also had a night shift, and one of the molders there was considered the crayon-making stud of that small but unique world. The night shift foreman told us about him and how many "pulls" he did in an evening, and I couldn't rest till I bested him. Without ever meeting or even communicating we fought back and forth for as long as there was a night shift, and finally I ended up ahead of him. I didn't get a raise for it. But the suits enjoyed looking at my numbers. They may have made the whole thing up, for that matter; I wouldn't put it past them.

I wasn't crazy about factory work; I don't think anyone is. So one morning I sought out the Naval Recruiting Office in a nearby large city. I couldn't find it, but perhaps subconsciously I really didn't want to. I did find the Marine Recruiting Office, but I wanted no part of them, having read casualty lists during World War Two. I went on back home and considered my situation, with which I was displeased. When I told The Brother that I was discontent with my lot, he replied, "Well, the thinking person usually is." I loved him for that.

College Again

Clearly, I had to get back to college, but there was little chance of it with my record as a goof-off. On the other hand, there was in my hometown a religiously oriented four-year college. I applied for admission. The factory gave me a dispensation, although the molders roasted me for aspiring to heights beyond my capacity.

I signed up for morning courses so I could keep working half-days. A World History course had some attractions, as well as a course in Journalism that focused on photography. Naturally I signed up for a course in Dramatics, I think it was called. Sounds like I was still in high school, doesn't it?

But this time I read the freaking books and went to all the lectures. I discovered that's how students passed courses and even got high grades. Lassie came home, and I got back on track. Three classes, two As and one B. And I didn't strain anything delicate.

I went so far as to appear in a stage production there, playing a lead in a historical drama. Can we say turgid? As we made up and got into costumes on opening night there came a knock at the door. One of the other actors answered it and then handed me a single rose. He said a young woman had brought one perfect rose for me. He raised hell with me about this, grumbling that no one ever brought him a perfect anything, let alone a rose. I told him he was too short, which he was. He would have hit the ceiling, but he couldn't reach it.

In fact, I knew the girl who brought the rose. Local guys nicknamed her The Biter because of her propensity to suck hickies on necks. It was worth it.

Back to the Factory

When the term ended and I returned to full time factory work the foreman asked me if I could type. I assured him I could; I'd had that course in high school. I wondered why he wanted me to type; perhaps to elevate me to an office job up front. Not a bit of it, they transferred me to the warehouse. When I made up orders to go out, they had to be labeled. The label-maker in no way resembled a typewriter.

During the rest of my twenty-seven-month sentence in that factory I did five-and-a-half day weeks in the warehouse. The crew and I spent happy hours piling outgoing boxes on wooden pallets. But we also unloaded semitrailers and boxcars filled with incoming materials, mostly wax and pigment. While the warehouse boasted air conditioning, as indeed the entire factory did, the semitrailers and boxcars didn't. And so it got middling warm in the summertime, and I never understood why the crayons didn't melt in such heat. But that wasn't my problem.

I didn't like the warehouse as much as I liked molding, but there were advantages. Every so often we would catch up with everything and all the orders and the foreman would tell us to go hide somewhere. Molders never got that opportunity.

Some diversions happened on Saturdays, when we only had to work until noon. The rest of the factory shut down on weekends, so on Saturday all incoming phone calls were directed to the warehouse. Often when one of us answered it would be because some little tyke somewhere had eaten some crayons. Frantic mothers would call for advice, and usually we told them to stay cool; this too would pass. But now and then someone would tell the panicky parent to rush the kid to the Emergency Room and have the little booger's stomach pumped. For all we knew, they did. I don't think the suits up front ever heard about any of this; at least we never had to appear in court, and no one got fired.

Every autumn we worked ten-hour days to keep ahead of the enormous demand for crayons and paints and such as the fall semesters/terms began to enroll little kiddies. More work, but more money, too, as we went on time and a half, or even double time on rare occasions, such as in the fall when the schools were opening and little children began to color bunny rabbits, autumn leaves, and such. Then the little darlings extorted enough cash from their parents to obtain boxes of anywhere from eight to one hundred and twenty-eight crayons. Those with the biggest boxes of crayons sniffed at those with lesser holdings. One did what one could with whatever one had. It was ever thus.

I vaguely recall having boxes of crayons in grade school, but they held little interest for me. I found out I could make green out of yellow and blue, and that sort of interested me, but beyond that I really didn't care.

Forklifts

We used forklifts in the warehouse, heavy little buggies with two tongs on the front that could be maneuvered with a hydraulic system. We used two-wheelers for light work, but the forklifts offered us salvation from back ruptures and hernias on heavier orders. Unloading or loading a boxcar or a semitrailer on a hot day is tough enough, but it went much faster if you could use a machine. We got to where we could insert the two tongs into a pallet with ease and aplomb, hoist up whatever it was and put it where someone else thought it should be. Who was I to argue?

A forklift, a chunky machine used to transport objects on wooden pallets. Their heavy weight kept them from turning over, and the barricade over the operator prevented items from falling down and killing him. I approved. From the author's collection.

Besides, I was dating, more or less, the foreman's daughter. Well, she often went to the midnight movie on Saturday night, and I couldn't let her walk back home. I mean, really. And I had a car by then.

The DumbAss

We had a DumbAss working in that factory, probably kin to the Fat Boy in The Country Grade School. We began to suspect him when he drove a forklift along the warehouse dock with his tongs so high that he broke out every light in the ceiling.

He confirmed our suspicions when he was asked to unload a boxcar full of supplies on pallets. Normal procedure required placing a bridge between the dock and the boxcar door, a sturdy bit of metal that supported the load either arriving or departing. But the DumbAss couldn't be bothered to go get the bridge; he thought he could jump his lift truck from the dock to the boxcar if he got up enough speed.

A forklift has a glide ratio about like Colorado, so his machine nosedived into the gap. Some other forklifts arrived with chains to pull him back onto the dock. The boxcar suffered substantial damage. The foreman reminded me of The Rancher as he speculated on the Dumb Ass's IQ and parentage.

One duty assigned to the DumbAss was to move full pallets of crayons from the molders to the labelers. Of course, one day he didn't get the forklift's forks in the pallet correctly and so dumped all eighteen boxes and thousands of crayons onto the floor.

He knew he'd done wrong and asked me what he should do. "Pick them up," I said, so he got busy picking up some 30,000 crayons about the time the Foreman arrived. They trashed the lot of them, and The DumbAss fell further into disfavor.

But the DumbAss reached his zenith as a pooch-screwer while I operated my mold. Across a wide aisle from the molds management stored stacks of barrels of pigment. These barrels weighed up to several hundred pounds, and thus required a forklift to move into position. The DumbAss was to replace the barrels at the appropriate molds. Could he screw this job up? Let me count the ways.

The DumbAss needed to keep pigment barrels in place for the molders, so he began to forklift a barrel of purple pigment into position. Alas, the barrels soared four stacks high, so he elevated his tongs to insert them in the pallet. But instead he inserted them into a barrel of purple pigment.

Pigment factories made purple from an extremely fine powder that flowed like water. When The DumbAss withdrew his tongs for another try the purple pigment spurted out, enveloping him in a large orchidaceous cloud.

By this time all the molders had stopped to enjoy the fiasco. Then bursting forth from the purple cloud emerged a shape, an even darker purple shape, that of The DumbAss with a pair of white eyeballs popping out of his head. That sight destroyed the molders altogether. The foreman appeared and we all got back to work, but The DumbAss spent the day cleaning up purple. He had a sort of purple haze about him as long as I knew him, rather like purple jaundice.

Departure

Even though the time just flew while I had such fun I left my hometown again, including The Factory. A few years later I had a summer off to prepare for matrimony, having secured two bachelor's degrees, one master's, and a fiancée. I could use some money, so I asked the Factory Foreman if he could use me for a couple of weeks. He said he always needed help in the warehouse, so I returned to the scene of past servitude.

The molders ragged me, of course, and asked me if that master's degree helped sweep the floor. I said it sure as hell did, because in two weeks I'd sweep out the door and into the parking lot and disappear, never to return. While they made crayons I would shape young minds.

So that hiatus ended, and I did lots better in college the second time around. I couldn't have done much worse. I taught a year of high school in a metropolitan slum, three years in a small college, and then successfully pursued a doctorate and got to play with the big boys.

But The Factory, like the Farm, had its impact on me. I never looked at a box of crayons quite the same way, just as I never liked Cokes very much after two weeks bottling them.

I also began to muse on the various factories that must exist in this world. Lots of people work in factories making automobiles, and that seems OK. So, too, with kitchen appliances or food processing plants. Somewhere factories turn out Vaseline by the ton, and somewhere else they spend all day making golf tees. Remember, I spent two weeks in a Coca-Cola bottling plant.

Somewhere in this favored land of ours, men dedicate their lives to making toilet paper. I'm glad they do, but I can imagine internecine warfare between the one-ply factions and the two-ply aficionados, to say nothing of the three-ply elitists.

They may even have a monthly newsletter or conventions of TP workers and administrators. I expect they'd have regional conventions as well as national. Perhaps they do international meetings. Guys lobbying other guys seeking professional advancement. Oh, God.

But facts are facts: The United States consumes over seven billion rolls of TP per annum. The average American uses 23.6 rolls per year. You could look it up. Rumor has it that Texans use more than people in other states.

But what of the sausage-makers? Or the places where workers make manhole covers? I drove by a factory once in which they made breakfast cereal; the stench would have made a hyena puke. Somewhere they manufacture whoopee cushions. I know there are places in which they artificially inseminate cattle and horses and I don't know what else. I don't want to know what else. Goats? Sheep?

Grown men and women sit around high-priced conference tables and try to figure out how to out-think a cat. I once bought a Christmas present for a couple of cats I know, a sort of feline-sized hammock. The packaging assured me that kitties loved it and would spend hours sprawled out in it. I had to get help assembling the damned thing, whereupon the two cats sniffed it once or twice, then ambled over to play with the empty box. I picked one up and put it on the hammock. She immediately got off and went to the basement. I surrendered.

CLICHÉ WARNING!!! CLICHÉ WARNING!!!

▼ ▼ ▼ ▼ ▼ ▼

"There are more things in heaven and earth, Horatio,
Than are dreamt of in your philosophy."
—*Hamlet*, Act I, Scene v, ll. 167-8

CHAPTER EIGHT

WHO CARES? AND, SO WHAT?

I headed back to The Teachers College, this time with more purpose. I read the textbooks; I attended the classes; and I made up for wasted time. The jock fraternity faded into oblivion, and I did my partying with my friends. We'd beer up; we'd read Pogo; that remained a constant, as did the Dawnbusters. I frolicked among the coeds until I came across one I wanted to live with. Our marriage lasted fifty-two years, and death did not us part. A doctorate seemed financially expedient, so I got one. Life became a lot different as I taught around the Midwest and even enjoyed one semester teaching in London. I retired in 1997. But I went back to The Little House on the Prairie, Part Three, now and then.

Homecomings

The Father retired from farming at age eighty-one. The Parents held a farm sale and converted what they could into cash, then moved into The Small Town Nearby.

I think that their generation, like all generations, felt a bit—what? Not frightened, exactly, but nonplussed by the technology their kids learned early. My son and I asked The Father what he thought about the Wright Brothers' flying when he read about it in 1903. He said he didn't believe it since the newspapers didn't have pictures. He lived to see the moon landing in 1969, at which point he exclaimed, "By God, that's enough!"

The Parents didn't grow up with electricity, telephones, automobiles, movies, television, or even radio. They had to learn how to use them as they went along. Sometimes they did; sometimes they didn't. The Mother was fifty before she ever had electricity, and it I think it made her uncomfortable, to say the least. She considered plugging something into every wall socket so no juice would leak out and get her, but we convinced her she didn't need to do that.

I sympathize with them; I recall sitting down to a computer the first time, for "the hands-on experience," as they called it. In time I found myself staring into glowing rectangles for a better portion of the day, and now the gurus threaten me with driverless cars. People on Mars. Virtual reality. Artificial intelligence. By God, that's enough!

The Parents experienced culture shock after they moved to The Little Town Nearby, to be sure; traffic noise at night kept them awake. Teenagers' hot rods didn't sound like coyotes. On the other hand, not having much to do brought them a sort of liberation, even if they resorted to daytime TV to fill their time.

The Brother lived nearby and looked after them faithfully. And The Sister visited, as did I. The Mother's sister, The Aunt, also moved to town, but to a different house. Neither woman would allow any assistance or interference with their housekeeping.

When I stayed with The Parents in town I would return now and then to that piece of prairie I once called home. My visits grew more and more depressing as the times changed. I changed, too.

The Abandoned Farm

Family farms have not disappeared completely from the Midwestern landscape, but very few remain. Farming came to demand enormous capital, more than a mere family could afford, and so conglomerates pretty much took over. I think that the rewards of farming became in no way commensurate with the effort required. We gained something with increased efficiency, but then too we lost something, something bucolic that had been of value.

Those few square miles I knew in the old days changed almost beyond recognition. Not the land, of course, but new owners tore down the Little House on the Prairie, Part Two, replacing it with a modern home. The outbuildings fell into disrepair and disappeared. Adolescent vandals burned down the stone barn, but I rescued a slab and imbedded it in my patio.

The Little House on the Prairie, Part Three, also came on hard times. Some strangers bought the farm, dragged in house trailers, and abandoned the Little House on the Prairie, Part Three. Time has eroded that house, and it won't last much longer. The barn has already caved in, literally; after sagging to the left for a decade it finally collapsed into rubble. The wooden silo is eroding from the top down, board by board. Many of the sheds and chicken houses disappeared, victims of entropy; a few remain. Unused machinery—pickups, tractors, graders, even that baler—rust where they were abandoned.

But by God you will search in vain for any horehound.

The creek where I spent so many hours goofing off has cut new channels. The bluffs seem much smaller now. So does everything else. I don't think any of those things got smaller, but I got bigger.

Our barn, which had been The Father's pride and joy, fell into disuse and collapsed when he sold his farm and moved into town. Photo by the author.

Lightning blasted the Little Country Grade School out of existence, but no one needed it after the grade schools consolidated. Whoever owned the land cleared it completely; not a shred of stone building, horse barn, johns, merry-go- round, or anything else remains. I rather miss it; I'd like to have seen it again. A poor thing, that school, but mine own.

They tore down the train station where we watched the Streamliner and from which we sent The Brother to World War Two. The Little Town Nearby has no rail passenger service nowadays.

People tell me nothing lasts forever. Even Bettie Page re-emerged briefly, then passed away, grieving thousands of dirty old men. During her renaissance she earned more money than she ever did when she dropped her laundry and cavorted for lechers, much good it did her. But I hold her memory in high regard; she gave me many moments of incandescent fantasy. Just last week, in fact.

So the beat went on, but I can still recall those simple country days before I made the break to high school and beyond. Do I remember them fondly? To a degree, perhaps, but I'm glad they ended. I didn't want to stay there to live with hogs and corn and chickens and cow-brutes and such. Not my scene, friends, I'd seen it up close and knew too much about it. But at the same time I felt a twinge of guilt that I didn't love it more.

I hope you don't want some sort of epiphany, because you won't get it. Time marched on with a capital T.

Showdown

So now we confront two questions essential to all narratives, two questions that I've printed out and framed to hang on a prominent wall in my study:

#1) Who cares?

#2) So what?

#1. I care, by God. I lived that simplistic life out there on the prairie, and I endured it, parts of it I even enjoyed, and now that sort of life has almost vanished. The majority of United States citizens lived in the country for quite a while, and that way forged a generation. A depression followed by a world war hardened the participants, and the survivors of those miserable times rescued civilization, no less. They whipped the Axis in World War Two and saved the world from fascism, and if that doesn't matter, what the hell does?

After all, there were definite advantages to living on a family farm in the old days. It was quiet, for one thing; I didn't realize how nice that was till I moved to town. And we had good food. And when the wind died down once or twice a year the air was clean and smelled wonderful. A field of freshly mowed alfalfa gives spiritual uplift to anyone passing by.

#2. So what? A harder cud to chew, that. It mattered to me; I wanted off that little world and an escape from dirt, beasts, and manure. I wanted that a whole lot, and I got it, sort of like that pickle back in Chapter One. So did lots of other country kids, after they'd failed at farming or grown sick of it.

And when I escaped, did I whimper and miss the farm? Surely you jest. True enough, I encountered other problems, problems of greater magnitude, but looking back I don't see any human endeavor this side of Pluto that isn't fraught with pitfalls.

You see, I finally realized I created my own problems, just like the rest of you. I could have become a cloistered monk with a vow of silence and done my time in a solitary cell and still found plenty of troubles.

How, I might hear you ask? Well, run down the list of the Seven Deadly Sins and see how many of them a person could do alone. Some encyclopedias suggest that each sin is a form of self-idolatry wherein the subjective reigns over the objective. I believe they've nailed it. OK, here they are: Pride, Greed, Lust, Envy, Gluttony, Wrath, and Sloth. Well, I never made any graven images.

If there exists on this planet any profession unpopulated by self-seeking and self-serving swine, I never found it. Higher education reeks with egos of galactic dimensions, clashing with one another like movie stars or operatic divas. As most professors maintain, academics fight so viciously because the stakes are so small.

Religion? The zealots seem to jockey for position and stab one another in the back, like congressmen. Consider the Crusades or the Spanish Inquisition. Art dealers and other curators of the humanistic deal regularly in hot properties and fake art works.

The military? When they run out of enemies they start shooting one another.

I could go on, but why bother? Even saints jostle with one another to emerge as the saintliest, don't they? They take pride in being the humblest? Do they have fistfights in Heaven about it?

So what? Did I learn anything along the way? Careening into senility, teetering on the brink of Old Timer's Disease, what do I know now that I didn't know then? Or do I merely suspect some things? Anything I want to pass on to anyone? I feel I must try.

High Point Finish

After Huck and Tom and Jim gave me such an excellent start I kept reading for the rest of my days, almost anything I could get my hands on, from Aristotle to cereal boxes to *The Story of O*. I thought maybe, just maybe, some dude or duchess might have discovered some practical advice on living and then written it down.

Sure enough, they had. Thousands of them. No two alike and most of them in conflict, often armed conflict. The same guys who discovered the true religion—several dozens of them–and the best way to run a society—another multitude–or the best medical treatments—many of which would kill you after they'd collected the fee—they all had the Revealed Word on how to live. And they would share that with you, if you could meet the price.

I grew wistful and discouraged when I would one day read Aristotle and learn from him that "Happiness is the meaning and the purpose of life, the whole aim and end of human existence," and the next day find Theodore Dreiser quoting an editor who shrieked out "Life is a God-damned, stinking, treacherous game and nine hundred and ninety-nine men out of a thousand are bastards."

But then I'd learn that madcap, fun-loving scamp, John Milton, suggested "The mind is its own place and in itself, can make a Heaven of Hell, a Hell of Heaven."

That's cool, but a French poet, Paul Valéry, took a different stance, suggesting:

> *Latent in every man is a venom of amazing bitterness, a black resentment; something that curses and loathes life, a feeling of being trapped, of having trusted and been fooled helpless prey of impotent rage, blind surrender, the victim of a savage, ruthless power that gives and takes away, enlists a man, drops him, promises and betrays, and—crowning injury—inflicts on him the humiliation of feeling sorry for himself.*

Jeez, Paul, lighten up. Try some decaf.

Another precinct was heard from when Thomas Hobbes offered his view of our earthly existence, stating: "the life of man, solitary, poor, nasty, brutish, and short." His wasn't all that short; he lived to about ninety. I just cannot recommend him too highly. In fact, I wish I hadn't mentioned him at all.

So the writers didn't know for sure, even the poets, although I dug it when Robert Frost said, "In three words I can sum up everything I've learned about life: It goes on."

But a couple of things stayed with me and have been some solace through the years. At best we are lazy, ignorant cowards. The price of love is loss, but time erodes pain. We are all creatures filled with imperfect virtues. Don't try to be what you're not. The more you cry the less you have to pee.

I guess I'm saying we each need to find focus. I read once that the purpose of life was to find a purpose in life. From the looks of it, not many people come into any sort of focus. I'm not sure I ever did. I had some help, though, some moments I didn't even recognize as they went by. When that high school agriculture teacher came out to rat on me for not taking his classes, only to be dismissed by The Father, that counted more than I knew at the time.

And when my high school buddy suggested we go try out for the junior high play, and I got cast in it and he didn't, that wrenched my life into a totally new direction.

Some books helped, little by little. Voltaire. Sophocles. Heinlein and Bradbury. Also jazz and Wagner and Beethoven; they all helped illuminate our condition, or at least mine. Eventually the Bard of Avon.

Marcus Aurelius, one of the good guys. His Meditations *I highly recommend. Many students of such matters especially praise the recent translation (2002) by Gregory Hays. I agree. From the author's collection.*

And Marcus Aurelius. Quite a group, is it not? I still read Marcus Aurelius every year, and he keeps getting smarter and smarter. He ruled the entire Roman Empire in his day, but he was still trying to figure out the best way to live. I remain impressed by him.

And some ideas stick. An interviewer once asked Tennessee Williams what he hoped people would gain, what they might think, what they might know, after seeing his plays. Williams took another slug of red wine, paused, and then drawled out, "Oh, I suppose that other people have been through it, too."

A little earlier Plato advised "Be courteous, for everyone you meet is fighting a hard battle." He got that right.

Delphi helped, too. Oh, Zeus, how it helped! You never know when the penny will drop, as the British say.

Delphi

One sunny day in 1970 I found myself on Mount Parnassus in Greece. Sunlight sparkled on the Saronic Gulf; eagles cavorted in the sky, and while standing in the ruins of the Temple of Apollo I said to myself, "My boy, you're a long way off the farm today."

Now, true, the idea that a Pythian oracle did her thing where I stood and answered questions to the supplicants who came there seeking help ranks right up there with The Tooth Fairy. The oracle spoke only gibberish, being stoned out of her mind from the vapors emanating from a fault line below her. The Apollonian priests would then have to decipher her predictions for those seeking answers. And did they charge for that service? Need you ask? Did they have prices for meals, housing, and purification rites? An airline couldn't have done it any better. And it sure beat farming.

I heard one bystander mutter, "Well, it makes as much sense as Easter." But I loved Delphi; indeed, I've asked that my ashes be scattered there for my final illegality.

Because on that temple, according to legend, on each end they inscribed a pithy saying.

The ruins of the Temple of Apollo at Delphi, Greece. The Pythian Oracle hung out here and answered questions put to her by people needing information about the future. Well, why not? Photo by the author.

On one pediment you could read "γνῶθι σεαυτόν (*gnōthi seautón* = "know thyself.") On the other they carved μηδέν ἄγαν (*mēdén ágan* = "nothing in excess.")

Nah, I don't speak or read classical Greek; I'm just hot-dogging here. But I suspect those old boys were on the right track. Moderation. Harmony. Strive, but stay cool about it.

We all have problems, not all of them our fault. Most, but perhaps not all. We all seek liberation, don't we? Liberation from what? Mostly, I fear, liberation from various virtues and self-made strictures. I believe comedy in fact frees us from lots of these, and leaves us exposed as our lewd, grinning selves.

And at the same time that we crave liberation we also crave power, to preserve our power, to exercise our power, to expand our power. This collision of desires results in a stacked deck. And all the art and science and philosophy cannot resolve it; you have to play the cards you're dealt, and that's all there is to that.

I've heard gamblers say one should always cut the cards. You won't win, but at least you'll last longer.

Henry Miller once addressed these issues. Sometimes Miller used pretty earthy language, causing some folks to brand him a pornographer. Usually the condemnations came from people who hadn't read his work, but this time he made his points very clearly indeed:

> *the struggle of the human being to emancipate himself, that is to liberate himself from the prison of his own making, that is to me the supreme subject.*

"Of his own making." The used copy in which I first read this passage had that phrase underlined.

When I read that I thought we can all whiz on the fire and call in the dogs; it's been said.

The search goes on for some sort of mindless euphoria, which we choose to call happiness. But I wonder if happiness isn't seeking us, rather than the other way around. Pat Conroy, in his blockbuster novel, *The Lords of Discipline,* suggests something like that:

> *I have come to distrust periods of extreme happiness and now when I discover myself in the middle of one, I glance nervously around me, examine all locks, cut back all the shrubbery around my house, avoid introductions to strangers, and do not travel on airplanes. Happiness is an accident of nature, a beautiful and flawless aberration.*

I think it's now time to shut down this Penny Dreadful. I wanted to preserve for a little the times in which as Twain once put it:

> *the charm and witchery and pathos which belong with the memories of a life that has been lived and will come back no more.*

THE END

ACKNOWLEDGEMENTS

Leading my list of folks to thank come the relatives, The Parents, who endured me those many years; the Sibs, who taught me everything from solitaire to inorganic chemistry, and all The Other Relatives.

An entire gaggle of teachers who tried to instill in me their appreciation of truth and commas. Overstreet. Walton. Shattuck. Hewitt. Some others.

Friends. The Trogdons. Sharon Hanson. The Krauses. Eva Marie Johnson. Many early readers.

Colleagues. Educators who labored in the same vineyards as I did and knew only too well what was going on. Good friends, many of them.

Computer gurus, who baled me out of my self-made messes too many times to count. Mr. George Kopp, the only person I know who can make a Macintosh computer execute an *entrechat.*

The family: Kelly and Steven

Authors traditionally confess that any errors in their work are their own, no one else's. That's only too true, but I'll treasure mine till the day I snuff it.

"I can no other answer make but thanks, and thanks, and ever thanks."

Twelfth Night, III, iii, 1503-4.

ABOUT THE AUTHOR

Stephen M. Archer resides in Columbia, Missouri, having retired from the University of Missouri in 1997 after twenty-seven years of teaching Theatre History, Playwriting, Graduate Research Methodology, and seminars ranging from The Structure of Comedy to Greek Tragedy to The History of Acting.

He now devotes his time to reading, writing, and musing over the vagaries of Macintosh computers.

He contemplates issuing more books and essays and such. He can be reached at archer.s.m@icloud.com. You may also order copies of this book from Amazon.com.

Made in the USA
Columbia, SC
26 August 2019